DO BUSINESS BETTER

"As a small business owner, I find myself sifting through business books seeking information that is realistic and relevant. While reading this book, I was able to take suggestions and apply them immediately. *Do Business Better* is helping my business successfully roll into our second decade."

—Angie Carel,
Owner of IBA Design

"Better always beats best, and this book will show you how you can get that competitive advantage. In this book, Damian Mason provides practical, actionable ideas you can use to better your best. I recommend it."

—Mark Sanborn, author,
The Fred Factor

"Common sense principles delivered in a no-holds-barred, Midwest farm boy conversational tone. If you have a profound desire to *Do Business Better* in a rapidly changing, disrupted, global economy, I wholeheartedly recommend you read a copy and share a few copies with your most valued clients or prospects!"

—Jamie Shinabarger,
President/CEO Springs Valley Bank & Trust

DO BUSINESS BETTER

Traits, Habits, and Actions
to Help You Succeed

DAMIAN MASON

WILEY

Published by John Wiley & Sons, Inc., Hoboken, New Jersey.
Published simultaneously in Canada.

For general information on our other products and services or for technical support, please contact our Customer Care Department within the United States at (800) 762-2974, outside the United States at (317) 572-3993 or fax (317) 572-4002.

Wiley publishes in a variety of print and electronic formats and by print-on-demand. Some material included with standard print versions of this book may not be included in e-books or in print-on-demand. If this book refers to media such as a CD or DVD that is not included in the version you purchased, you may download this material at http:// booksupport.wiley.com. For more information about Wiley products, visit www.wiley .com.

Library of Congress Cataloging-in-Publication Data:

Names: Mason, Damian, 1969- author.
Title: Do business better : traits, habits, and actions to help you succeed / Damian Mason.
Description: Hoboken, New Jersey : John Wiley & Sons, Inc., [2019] | Includes index. |
Identifiers: LCCN 2018061444 (print) | LCCN 2019003661 (ebook) | ISBN 9781119566298 (Adobe PDF) | ISBN 9781119566304 (ePub) | ISBN 9781119566281 (cloth)
Subjects: LCSH: Success in business. | Management.
Classification: LCC HF5387 (ebook) | LCC HF5387 .M3475 2019 (print) | DDC 650.1—dc23
LC record available at https://lccn.loc.gov/2018061444

Cover Design: Wiley

Printed in the United States of America.

V10008340_022119

Contents

Foreword

It is my firm belief that people want both life and business to be hard so they will have an excuse for not doing well. After all, who wants to admit failure at something that is really pretty simple, right? But the reality is that life just isn't all that hard. Neither is business. Sure, it can be difficult from time to time, and disasters may happen along the way. But for the most part, when you boil it all down, success in both life and business is really based on some pretty simple, basic stuff. "It" isn't hard, but we sure seem to enjoy making it hard and believing it's hard.

It has been my experience that the reason most people aren't as successful as they want to be is that they never learn or they too quickly forget the simple, basic principles it takes to do well. Then when they struggle in either their life or their business, they go searching for answers and will invariably gravitate toward intricate, complicated solutions. Interesting approach, since what got them into trouble in the first place wasn't intricate or complicated at all; it was the lack of application of simple, basic principles. Want to lose weight? Eat less, exercise more. That is a simple solution that works 99% of the time. But people don't want that solution; they would rather spend money on silly ideas like an Ab Cruncher or a pill promoted by a celebrity. That's why the weight loss industry is a $66 billion industry. Eating less and exercising more won't cost you a dime, but the solution just seems too simple and basic for people to accept.

Even when people are doing well but want to do better, they skip the simple, basic stuff that would help them do better and go for the complicated, sexier stuff that seems to be all the rage. Business books have become more and more about offering complex solutions to simple problems. Authors know that few people really want to be reminded about getting back to basics. People believe they are already doing the basics well enough and want what's hot and is the flavor of the day. Well, what's hot is rarely the solution to the problem. The problem, 9 times out of 10, was caused because the basics were ignored.

That's what I enjoy most about *Do Business Better;* it's about the basics. That's even what I like best about the title. The title doesn't promise you anything grandiose like how you will become the biggest, the best, or the richest. And it isn't one of those silly titles we see way too often that is hard to understand, with ideas inside that are even harder to implement. The title of this little book is basic and reminds us of what we all ultimately want: the ability to do business better. The content inside is the same way. This book gives you solid, basic ideas that will show you how to do business better. And if you are honest with yourself, that is what you are really looking for. You aren't looking to totally overhaul what got you where you are. That's too big of a task, and you aren't going to do it anyway. What you really want is a handful of ideas, strategies and tactics that will help you tweak what you are doing today so you can do business better tomorrow. And the simpler to implement, and the fewer of them there are, the better.

And that's exactly what Damian delivers. He gives you solid, tactical, simple, easy-to-implement ideas that will help you do business better so you can enjoy your life with fewer headaches, less frustration, and end up with more money in the piggy bank. What more could you ask for?

I've known Damian for many years. We have sat on each other's patio and talked about every topic under the sun. We have probably shared a thousand cigars and more than a few drinks kicking around ideas on business, life, money, aging, relationships, politics, dogs, and other things I am unwilling to mention here. Damian is a successful speaker, farmer, and businessman. In all of our many hours of conversation, we have laughed about how difficult people make things, when it simply isn't necessary. Damian, like me, can attribute all of his success to excelling at the simple, basic stuff. Nothing fancy and nothing that anyone else couldn't do if they would just get out of their own way and do the work. That's why we get along so well. We agree that success is attainable for all willing to get back to basics and do the work.

Damian has a sharp mind and a sharper tongue. He is fun to talk to, and I get a kick out of how his mind works. His stuff is also fun to read and you will enjoy his writing, his humor, and the great ideas that will help you do business better.

Larry Winget

Introduction

I Get You

I wrote this book for you. You, the aspiring entrepreneur, budding businessperson, or established business owner pursuing growth.

I understand you because I am you. When I resigned from corporate America to command my own ship, I needed this book. Just like you do.

You've read business books. You've seen the flowery fluff. You've studied (or tried to) the books of platitudes telling you to keep a positive mental attitude.

Now it's time for you to put some meat in your diet of entrepreneurial learning. This book is your reality burger.

Let's Talk About *You*

You're overwhelmed. Your suppliers frustrate you. So do your employees. Sometimes your customers do, too.

Or maybe you're still working a normal job and your co-workers frustrate you. Because you're not like them. You don't want to die in a job you hate.

You think about money. Even when times are good. Because you've endured several months when finances were a struggle. You're willing to make financial sacrifices now for a greater financial reward in the future.

Your creativity isn't stoked in your current capacity. Or maybe you run your own business and you struggle to find time for creative indulgence.

You are your company's best salesperson. It'd be fantastic if sales doubled and you could raise your prices. Your less inventive competitors cheapen the market.

Sometimes you're tempted to throw in the towel and give up on being your own boss. But your independent side won't let you. You have goals. Frankly, you've already achieved more than most people thought you would when you announced your intentions years ago.

Maybe you're on the cusp of launching your endeavor. You don't tell your peers of your intention. You don't want to hear them doubt you and your abilities.

You know success is attainable. Naysayers annoy you. You want more for yourself than others want for themselves. This doesn't make you greedy; it makes you a minority. Because you're actually willing to work for it.

You've failed before. Probably a few times. But you learned from failure. You learn best from the lessons you pay for and you view your failures as the price of tuition. Your stumbles taught you that strivers are judged by those who've never even made an attempt.

You think about work and business a lot. You like how you feel when you've been productive. You relish the sense and feel of accomplishment.

I'm guessing multiple statements in the above paragraphs accurately describe you.

While others may not understand you or your ambition, I get you. I want you to prosper by doing business better.

Trying versus Doing

If you believe it *is* possible to create the life and business of one's choosing, you're in the right place. To accomplish this, you must *do*, not *try*.

Everyone's "trying" to do something, aren't they? Broke people are "trying" to save money. Bad parents are "trying" to spend more time with their kids. Dissatisfied employees are "trying" to find a fulfilling job. Some of those dissatisfied employees are "trying" to start their own business.

Understand this: "Try" is bullshit.

"Try" is what weak people say when they mean "no."

"Try" is what underachievers say when they seek credit for doing something they didn't do.

"I'll try to make it" means "I'm not coming but instead of saying 'no' I'll say 'try' to avoid hurting your feelings."

"I'll try to get your project done" means "I am lazy and won't work on any of this but I fear you'll yell at me so I'm lying instead."

This book isn't titled "TRY to Do Business Better." It's titled "DO Business Better."

That's intentional.

Invest a Couple Hours, Then *Do It!*

I know your time is valuable. You're working a job and contemplating a jump off the high dive. Maybe you're already swimming in the deep end known as business ownership. Either way, you have plenty of demands on your schedule.

This book will take you no more than a few hours to complete. The applicable takeaways will save you months of frustration. Maybe even years. From a time investment standpoint, that's one helluva ROI!

There are short, simple exercises within many of the chapters. Do them. It'll make you stronger.

The goal: to accentuate your traits, implement habits, and take actions that allow you to prosper.

When you're finished with this book, you'll know:

- The traits of entrepreneurial success and how to tap into yours.
- Success habits to intentionally develop.
- Actions that lead to prosperity.
- How to exploit and expand upon your strengths.
- How to create a life and business by choice!

Are you ready to Do Business Better?

1

Success Defined.
By You.

Success Is Different for Everyone

In the pages that follow you're going to see a lot of references to success. As you would in any business or self-help book. Remember, there's big money to be made in telling people they can be successful. Particularly if you tell people no effort is required, other than buying what the success peddler is selling, of course!

I won't tell you success is easy. I won't tell you it requires no effort. Success requires effort. Success also requires changing what you're currently doing or how you're doing it.

Before we roll into how you can succeed, let's first define success.

Hint: Yours is the only definition that matters.

Ask 100 people what success means to them and you'll get 100 different responses. There's the superficial—a Lamborghini in the driveway or a mansion with boats and jewelry. Then there's the more spiritual concept of contented peacefulness. Maybe for the family-oriented sort, success is all about time with loved ones.

You're entitled to whatever mental picture of success you want. What matters is that you possess a mental picture of success. Also, it's okay if that picture of success changes over time. That's called growth. It's good to let your vision of success evolve. It's bad when your picture of success changes because you simply gave up.

Your Evolving View of Success

As a 20-year-old, I thought success was a Mustang 5.0 convertible with a "DAMIAN" vanity plate. I toiled as a factory worker and laborer with that view of me someday hitting the zenith of accomplishment.

Then I grew up and it dawned on me: I'm not in a 1980s rock-and-roll video. I don't comfortably fit in that era of Mustang. And I don't need a vanity plate to make me any more identifiable.

The point: As you mature, your picture of success will be slightly different from what it was at age 20. Today I could have a garage full of 1988 Mustangs. All with personalized license plates. But I no longer deem that the picture of success.

Things change. Life events cause change. Hopefully, you as a person are changing (for the better!). The crucial element to success isn't that the picture stays the same. What's crucial is that you don't throw in the towel and just accept mediocrity.

You know people like that and so do I. It's pathetic. You watch them underachieving, making no effort. All the while they're lying to themselves, pretending it's what they've always wanted.

It's acceptable for your definition of success to evolve. Unless evolution means giving up.

"I Just Want to Be Happy!"

Several of those 100 respondents we hypothetically asked, "What does success look like to you?" will answer: "I just want to be happy."

When I hear people say this, I honestly think about hitting them with an axe handle. My dog "just wants to be happy," too. You're a grown-up and a human. You are in charge of your life, much as many people pretend otherwise, thereby avoiding responsibility for the outcome. Saying "I just want to be happy" won't make you happy. Happiness is an active choice and generally requires doing something with purpose.

So it goes with success. How you define it is up to you. The important step is that you *do* define it. Then burn a picture in your brain of what it looks like. That picture of success in your head is where you're going. Success, as defined by you, is your journey and your destination. Do you see it?

To Help You Out, Here's My Definition of Success

Each day, doing more of my choosing, and less that is imposed upon me. With financial resources to do so. Actively, enjoyably, and flavorfully.

My version of success involves working. I enjoy productivity. But increasingly, I want it to be on my conditions. That's where the money comes in. Not for vanity license plates, but for the choice it affords me. Lastly, success to me is being physically active until death, with my wife and dog, then enjoying tasty food, beer, and cigars at the end of the day.

To me, working and living on one's own terms, *is* success. Is there more? What does your mental picture of success look like?

What's your definition of success?

_____

_____

_____

2 Get Better

I had a role years ago in a fairly forgettable movie titled *2001: A Space Travesty*. If you're really bored some day, order it up and watch it. Don't do it for my benefit, though—I don't get residual payments!

The film starred Leslie Nielsen. I have 40 minutes of screen time, which puts me loosely in a supporting actor role. While filming a scene, Mr. Nielsen gave me some input.

"Damian, do you want to be a successful actor?"

"Yes, sir," I replied.

"Then I've got two words of advice for you: Get better."

The cast and crew got a good laugh at the famous actor's wisecrack. But Mr. Nielsen's point is valid, comedy aside. If you want to be successful at acting—or anything—get better.

I'm really not an actor. Yes, I have Screen Actors Guild membership and yes, I've been paid to act in several productions. But there's slim chance you'll ever see a Damian Mason star on the Hollywood Walk of Fame. That's fine with me.

I did take Leslie Nielsen's advice. At that point in my life and career, I was being paid to act. Being paid to do something makes you a professional. Therefore, my business was acting. So, I made it my business to get better at my business.

I studied the methods and habits of seasoned actors who were on set with me. During slow spells between filming, I sought training from my more experienced co-stars. By the way, if you've never been involved in movie production, it's almost entirely slow time between filming! I utilized that slow time to do business better.

This book is all about doing business better. For that to happen, *you* must get better. Maybe you've been in business a long time. Or maybe you're still an employee plotting your entrepreneurial venture. Either way, you can always improve.

It's been 20 years since I was in front of the camera with Leslie Nielsen. At least once a week I recall those words. I apply the simple advice to everything I do. Want to be successful? *Get better*!

I Didn't Say Get Perfect

Notice I did not say, "Get perfect"? I said, get better.

Perfect means without flaws, defects, or shortcomings. Sound like anyone you know? Businesses are owned and staffed with humans. Businesses profit by serving humans. There is no such thing as a human without flaws, defects, or shortcomings. That's why better is a more practical objective than perfect.

Perfect Isn't Profitable

If you wait until your product is perfect, you'll never sell any product. That's why you receive recall notices on cars you own. They sell them before they're perfect.

Lexus once had an advertising slogan touting "the relentless pursuit of perfection." But they never claimed their cars *were* perfect. They just claimed they were "pursuing" perfect. Certainly, Lexus makes a nice automobile. But management doesn't hold cars in the factory until they're perfect or they'd be bankrupt. The same goes for your company.

Perfection Is Unattainable

Perfect is unattainable. You might argue by telling me your daughter received a perfect test score. Okay. Yes, perfect scores are attainable. In scholastics! Now convert her test score into a business. There are vast differences between business and academia. (Please don't get me started here!). Businesses have to make money selling products and services. Perfect products and services don't exist.

Lack of Perfection Doesn't Mean Lack of Performance

My Nissan Maxima isn't perfect. Heck, Nissan doesn't even pursue perfection! Their advertising touts "innovation that excites." Yet, my Nissan performs remarkably well, despite its imperfections. Incidentally, it's not that exciting either, contrary to its marketing.

You can be amazingly successful selling good, but not perfect, products that perform. Truth is, the marketplace doesn't even expect perfect. Because almost nothing is!

Look at swimmer Michael Phelps, the most decorated athlete in Olympic history. Winner of 28 medals, 23 of which are gold. I'm willing to bet Michael Phelps would analyze his gold medal performances and point out flaws. Maybe his turns were less fluid than ideal or his dive entry was off a smidge.

That's right, the best swimmer in the history of sport would likely tell you his competitive swims were slightly imperfect.

You can always find a defect or a shortcoming. By all means, work to correct your flaws. That's what getting better is all about. But if you wait until you, your product, and your business are perfect, you'll die before you ever turn a nickel.

"Better" is attainable. "Better" is profitable. "Perfect" isn't necessary.

1

Traits

3 Four Unwavering Traits of Entrepreneurial Success

Several years ago I was a guest at a high school entrepreneur class. It was eye opening. The students were learning textbook stuff straight out of their curriculum. Their instructor was a career schoolteacher whose parents were retired schoolteachers. With a pedigree like that, is it any wonder this entrepreneur class didn't become a startup incubator?

During the guest lecture, the students asked me, "What is required to succeed running one's own business?"

Before answering, I turned the question back on them. Most of the students believed a solid business plan was the critical requirement. After all, that's what they'd been taught.

I told the students the same thing I'm going tell you. Textbooks are fine. Education is important. But business plans are completely overrated, probably even unnecessary.

Success running one's own business comes from developing good habits and possessing four traits. Here then are the Four Unwavering Traits of Entrepreneurial Success:

1. Risk Tolerance
2. Drive
3. Resilience
4. Vision

You needn't be self-employed to benefit from these traits. Nor do all small business operators possess them. But it's guaranteed the more these characteristics define you, the more prosperous your enterprise will be.

Good News, Bad News

To a certain degree, these characteristics are learnable. To a certain degree, they're not.

I'll use comedy as an example.

I've said forever, being funny is like being tall—you either are, or you are not, and it'll be obvious to everyone by the time you're an adult.

Yes, I've studied the craft of making people laugh. I completed improvisational comedy classes at Second City. I've read books by great comedians. I've studied the tactics of humor.

In spite of this, I believe it's impossible to teach someone to be funny. However, if you're already funny, you can learn to be funnier. I've been funny since childhood. Through diligence and learned techniques, I got funnier.

Point: You can train a funny person to be hilarious. But all the training in the world won't turn a librarian into a comedian.

It's Who You Are

Like comedy, you can learn elements of the four traits. However, at some fundamental level, you must possess these traits or you'll struggle as your own businessperson.

You wouldn't have picked up this book if you didn't have entrepreneurial spirit. Therefore, I'm guessing you already possess a certain degree of the four traits. But the goal is to do business better. Which means we need to dig a little deeper and try a little harder. Some of this may get uncomfortable. That's okay. No great improvement ever came about without a certain amount of discomfort.

Let's get started.

4

Risk Tolerance

In the interest of time (yours), I'll lay it on the line right up front: If the mere thought of not having a guaranteed paycheck, for a guaranteed amount of money, causes you to break out in hives, stop reading. You have no business running your own business.

For the rest of you who are staying the course, here's the good news: There's no such thing as a career with a guaranteed paycheck for a guaranteed amount of money, though government employment comes really close.

Now let's talk about you, your business, and the reality of risk.

Rose-Colored Lenses

Allegedly, there was a time in America when you were hired by a company, then retired from the same organization 40 years later. I say "allegedly" because my entire working life I've heard people harken for the "good old days."

Like the 1950s, for example. They were amazing times. Just ask anyone who lived back then. It was so wholesome back in the "good old days." They drove '57 Chevys to the sock hop where they kicked off their saddle shoes and danced. Except for the kids who were crippled by polio. Or the black kids who weren't allowed to attend.

The good old days weren't as good as we like to pretend they were.

In my speaking career, I've talked to a vast array of industries. Regardless of what these people do, it's always the same story: "Damian, our industry is going through a lot of change. Back when I started, it wasn't like this. Nowadays, it's gotten really competitive. . . . Blah blah blah."

I've been hearing about the good old days of 30 years ago for 30 years. It's all bunk! Do you truly believe that only a few decades ago you showed up at your job, then customers came in and tossed dollar bills at you? There is only one profession where that happens. And even those professionals don't work with any guarantee—eventually their economy is going to sag, too!

There Has Always Been Risk

Just like the good old days weren't always good, there has always been risk. Personal, financial, and professional.

Personal Risk

Living is risky. Why do you think 60% of Americans have life insurance? Because people know they might suddenly die. So they pay for something they hope to never use, thereby minimizing long-term risk.

Your personal risk varies by where and how you live. Certain activities present more inherent downside—skydiving versus dominoes, for example. Sure, people die playing dominoes but that's due to old age, not because their chute didn't open.

Financial Risk

There's risk in investing your money. Always has been. A century ago, your savings account wasn't even safe. Hence, bank runs during the Great Depression. Stock market, real estate, cryptocurrency, grain futures. . . . Any place you can put money has potential for peril. Even cash in the mattress or coins buried in a Mason jar aren't safe. What if the bedroom catches on fire or you forget where you buried the Mason jar?

Risk is why you earn interest, dividends, or appreciation. Financial return is compensation for the uncertainty.

Professional Risk

So it is with your business. You should demand financial compensation for putting yourself on the line and running your own business.

Companies go out of business every day. People go broke every minute. In 2017 there were 800,000 bankruptcies in the United States and that's almost half what it was during the Great Recession. This ain't no cakewalk!

You seek to create the life and business of your choosing. Everyone will tell you they want that, too. The reason most never attain it is because they don't possess the moxie, which is to say, they can't get beyond the risk to achieve it. Deep down they know this about themselves. They're scared.

> Those with no stomach for risk play it safe their whole career, then call those who didn't "lucky."

Risk, Reward, and Richard

As a teenager I had a part-time job for a local business owner. Richard had his hand in several entities, none of which you'd call glamorous. Moving dirt, a stone quarry, storage units, a roller rink, and even portable toilets.

He didn't start with all that. He started with a dump truck and a backhoe.

Richard had some low scrubland behind the shop. He also had construction jobs where excess dirt needed to be removed. His answer: use someone else's dirt they're paying to have removed for your own benefit. He filled in the low, unusable ground and built storage units there. His office manager rented the storage units.

Richard saw a need for portable toilets, likely because he worked on a lot of job sites. His answer: buy and rent "porta-johns." Presumably, his first client was himself. Then developers on his job sites. That grew into private parties—and anyone else long on people and short on bathrooms.

He had just purchased a small stone quarry when I worked for him. Job sites need sand and gravel. Richard became vertically integrated, supplying his own raw materials.

In the 1970s, before I was an employee, roller skating reemerged in popularity. Richard knew about site development because of his other business. So he built a roller rink. Throw in some cool lights, a DJ booth, a snack bar, along with skate rentals, and you have a business. One that employed his children, taught them a work ethic, and diversified the empire.

Huge corporations have the luxury of hiring researchers. Richard didn't. You don't either.

Richard didn't hire exploratory committees to offer opinions on the viability of his ventures. But he observed needs in the marketplace and took a risk to satisfy the need. The reward: a business success story.

You're a small businessperson. While you can't just shoot from the hip and hope everything works out, you will advance through smart risk. And effort, of course.

Where do you observe a need?

More importantly, what ventures could you take on that complement your current business?

Can You Stomach the Risk?

The first question I ask businesspeople I work with is, "What's your risk tolerance?"

Can you go a year without making money? During that time, can you sleep at night while your life savings are at risk to keep you afloat? Does uncertainty leave you unsettled? How unsettled? Up to this point in your life, how have you handled adversity?

There's a good chance your risk aptitude is consistent in all three categories—personal, financial, and professional. But not necessarily. The main thing is that you know yourself and your threshold for uncertainty.

A Matter of Scale

Neat thing about life, there's always someone that's more of something than you. Someone richer, poorer, smarter, dumber, tougher, weaker, and so on. Same with acceptance of risk.

There are people so risk averse they make you look like a daredevil. On the other hand, there are extreme risk takers who make you look chicken.

Evel Knievel and the Reality of Risk

Success comes from knowing when to be a daredevil and when to play chicken. You don't always have to go all in like the renegade at the poker table. Sometimes it's wise to play it safe. Other times, you need to pull out your inner Evel Knievel.

If you don't know who Evel Knievel is, I'm sorry. Not for my reference but for your loss. Evel was a stunt performer, known for amazing motorcycle jumps, lots of injuries, and an attempted rocket jump over Snake River Canyon.

I had Evel Knievel toys as a child. He is my vision of the ultimate risk taker. A pretty darn good promoter, too.

How to Minimize Risk

Want the good news? You needn't be an Evel Knievel to be successful. Although you should take a marketing lesson from the iconic daredevil.

Business prosperity doesn't require you to jump a row of buses on a Harley. But it does require risk.

The other good news: Risk can be minimized. Although never fully mitigated. Here's how you reduce the likelihood of bad outcomes for yourself and your enterprise.

Competence Breeds Confidence

Skill, knowledge, and experience are always in demand. Assuming, of course, your skill, knowledge, and experience are relevant to the marketplace. Being highly skilled at VCR repair won't fetch you much monetary reward these days.

When you know what you're doing, risk is reduced. To reach the point where you know what you're doing, you need to have actually done something. Probably failed a few times, too.

Failure teaches us more than success if we're willing to take the lesson.

Take Mr. Knievel. He started doing motorcycle stunts as a teenager. In fact, it was the Butte, Montana police department who nicknamed 16–year-old Robert Craig Knievel Jr. "Evel." It was right after arresting him for reckless driving.

When it came to riding—and flying—a motorcycle, Knievel was competent. Crazy, perhaps, but competent. Due to much experience. What do you suppose gave Evel more wisdom? The hundreds of successful stunts or the dozen crashes?

Hard Workers Seldom Starve

When I started my own venture, concerned people asked, "What will you do if this doesn't work out? Showbiz is difficult!"

It was clear these people had never taken a chance on anything. It also occurred to me, I'd been working since age 8. If the showbiz endeavor flopped, I'd simply go to work doing something else. But not until I'd applied every ounce of effort and work ethic toward my own venture first.

A willingness to work puts risk in perspective. When you're a hard worker, you always know, deep down, you'll be fine.

The prospect of risk shouldn't faze a go-getter. Conversely, a lot of risk avoiders are what you might politely call "Non Go Getters."

Taking Risk Off the Table

Your business is chugging. But there are no guarantees it'll continue. What do you do to minimize the downside? Take risk off the table where you can. Here's how:

- **Avoid debt**: We'll talk more about this in the Money chapter but it's worth repeating. You can't have a life and business of your choosing if you're beholden to creditors. Indebtedness spikes your stress level when combined with the inherent risk of running your business.
- **Insurance**: The world's a risky place. Insure against it where feasible. Being well insured will free up your mind to run your business knowing you and your loved ones are covered in the event of catastrophe.
- **Multiple income streams**: Your business revenue isn't guaranteed. Supplemental income from other sources lowers exposure to any one category.
- **Forward Thinking**: Marketplaces change. To avoid risk of obsolescence, stay in front of it. What can you implement today to satisfy a need tomorrow?

What About Backup Plans?

I don't believe in having a lot of backup plans. Here's why: When you give yourself too many fallback options, you're never fully committed to your original objective.

Yes, your business should evolve. Don't confuse evolution with changing directions every two weeks because you hit a snag.

It's normal to ask the question, "What if?" Just understand that every alternative path you focus on subtracts energy from where you're going.

Don't Sweat It

The reality: Running your own business is a challenge. But it's probably less perilous than you think. Especially if you know yourself and your tolerance for risk. Do you?

Gut Check

Are you a scaredy cat or an Evel Knievel? There's no shame. No one will see this answer but you. What is your risk-taker rating?

(Scaredy Cat) 1—2—3—4—5—6—7—8—9—10 (Evel Knievel)

How long did it take you to circle a number? Personally, I thought about this for quite a long time. I'm probably a low 8. The side of me that came from nothing who's now worth something will no longer allow me to risk everything.

There's no right answer. The idea was to make you think about your ability to function under varying levels of risk and stress.

Before we move on to the next chapter, a little inspiration as it pertains to risk and reward.

Angie

You don't know Angie but if you follow me on social media or visit my website, you've seen her work. Angie is my go-to for design, layout, print, promotional

(*continued*)

(continued)

products, marketing, social media, and a few more things I'm probably forgetting. She helps my business.

Angie and I have been working together for years. When we met, she was a designer for an organization of which I was a client. She and I both left for the same reason—her boss was an incompetent jackass.

Months later, I needed help and she needed income. Turns out there were a couple of other small-businesspeople in the same boat. Angie started her own company. With four clients. She was a mother of three and going through a divorce at the time.

Her business has grown from a young woman working from the kitchen table in a rental house to a sleek office with several employees. She has a thriving business she built from nothing but ambition and a handful of relationships.

Did she worry about how things might pan out? Probably. Probably still does occasionally. Everyone who steers their own ship worries at some point. But you can't let worry consume you. You'll never get ahead by constantly festering over the "what-ifs."

Here's the Point

There are no perfect times or can't-miss opportunities to start your own endeavor. You can always make an excuse, put off your ambition, or say, "Now's not the time." Angie sought creativity. She envisioned a business working on her terms.

Sure, she could have stayed where she was, working for the incompetent jackass. That would have been the safe thing to do. The easy, unfulfilling, unhappy, path of least resistance thing to do. But she didn't. Because Angie wanted her own business and was willing to take the risk to make it happen. She's a pretty ambitious gal too, which brings us to our next chapter.

5 Drive

Now we're covering a trait everyone can learn but many choose not to: drive.

Call it drive, ambition, or work ethic. You'll find it's a standard ingredient in successful people.

Potential to Do What?

Ever hear an idea or person described as having "a lot of potential"? It's a common statement. The only problem is that potential has no value until it actually turns into something. Tell the grocery store you have a lot of potential you'd like to exchange for food. Try paying your mortgage with potential.

Everything has potential. My farmland has potential to produce crops, timber, hay, and, beef. But without diligent effort and management, the farm yields very little.

So it is with people and businesses.

Drive Equals Discipline

I have no idea whether or not you're a go-getter. But you better know whether or not you are. Starting, running, and growing a business requires effort. Generally of the self-starting variety.

Don't despair; remember I told you drive was learnable? It is.

Drive is simply discipline. There's no such thing as an "ambition gene." Ambitious people are just more disciplined. Driven people work even when they don't want to. They work harder, smarter, and longer. Driven people possess the fortitude to focus on the end result.

Everyone has potential. Discipline turns that personal potential into results.

Most of what it takes to succeed boils down to a willingness to work. Most of work ethic simply boils down to discipline.

Talent Without Discipline Is Just Potential

My old friend and college roommate—we'll call him Woody—was comedically brilliant. Presumably, he still is. I don't know; we haven't talked in years. Woody got increasingly difficult to be around as we aged, mostly because of resentment.

You see, Woody is a smart guy, with incredible wit and comedic talent you can't teach. But he never became a professional comedian. I did. Therein lies the rub. He also spent a couple years describing himself as a writer when, in reality, he was a waiter. He was off by one letter!

Woody is an immensely talented guy. His limitations were being irresponsible and professionally undisciplined.

We all know people like Woody. Right now you're thinking of someone you know who possesses God-given talent you'd pay for, who's doing absolutely nothing with said talent.

I secretly used to worry I wasn't talented enough to make it in showbiz. Then it became apparent: there are lots of people with talent, but few people with a work ethic.

Talent is useless until it delivers something of value to a paying customer. And the only way talent delivers value is through disciplined application of the talent.

> Talent is useless until it delivers something of value.

Teaching a Work Ethic

I'm often told how fortunate I am to have grown up on a dairy farm. The farm taught me a work ethic, they say. That's true. But learning a work ethic isn't like learning arithmetic. There's no textbook, theorems, or final exam. You learn a work ethic by working.

Speaking of the farm, my wife, Lori, and I are occasionally hit up by acquaintances who want us to hire their children. "I'd like Junior to learn a work ethic. . . . Would you hire my kid to work on your farm?"

What these people are really saying is, "I'm a lazy parent with a lazy kid because I never make Junior do anything. Will you be the heavy?"

Lori and I have honestly discussed charging for this service.

Parents, your children learn what you teach them, including a work ethic. At age 8, I had real responsibilities. Caring for livestock and making hay was the family business. Our liveli-hood depended on getting those tasks completed. Every day.

From this, I learned the effort required to finish a job. I know the satisfaction that comes from putting tons of hay in the barn. Do you? Do your kids? You do your offspring a disservice by shielding them from effort.

> Don't confuse "drive" with being busy, waking up early, or spending lots of time at the office.

Activity versus Productivity

Ask anyone and they'll tell you how hard or how much they work. It's also a tradition for older generations to gripe that the younger generation is unmotivated. The younger end of the millennial generation is getting a lot of flack at the moment. I don't know if these kids are slackers or not. I'm still stuck on the fact that they won't eat bread because they fear gluten, yet they ingest Tide pods.

Back to the subject of drive: Productivity—not activity—is the measuring stick that matters. Contrary to popular belief, the world doesn't care how "busy" you claim to be.

Lots of people are busy. Just ask them. No, don't. You won't have to because they'll tell you. Repeatedly.

Don't confuse busy with productive. There are people who buzz like bees from sunup to sundown, yet accomplish nothing.

To break the busy habit, list outcomes you want. Prioritize them. Post them on a bulletin board or whiteboard. Every day, apply focused effort toward completion.

Businesspeople get paid for results, not for being busy.

Wake-Up Time Is Meaningless

Right up there with self-proclaimed busy people are those who equate wake-up time with productivity. They're wrong. Results matter. Wake-up time doesn't.

We all know people who wake up early. I swear some people do this just so they can tell everyone what time they get up.

As a sales rep, I traveled with a regional manager occasionally. One morning in a Marriott, he told me, "You know which rooms are occupied by hard workers. Their newspaper isn't lying in front of their door after 6 a.m."

There is scant logic behind this, of course. What if the hotel occupant was up late signing a million-dollar contract with a client? Or what if the room occupant was on the phone making sales calls that morning instead of reading the paper?

My manager was a former military guy who placed a high value on wake-up time. So, when traveling with my Marine boss, I adapted. I woke up every morning at 5:00, at which time I used the restroom, removed the newspaper from in front of my door, and went back to bed for a few hours.

Success doesn't care what time you wake up. There are plenty of unproductive early risers.

Hours Don't Equal Output

Most people overstate how many hours they work. If you bill your customers by the hour, it's good for revenue to log a lot of hours. If you're not, or even if you are, focus on output per hour rather than simply time spent.

Working Smart versus Working Hard

I worked hard growing up on the farm. Although I can't say it was always the smartest allocation of resources. Physical labor taught me a work ethic. It also taught me the value of working smart versus working hard.

Look at your business. Are you breaking your back? Working hard when you could be more productive by working smart?

People who run their own business struggle with where to apply their drive. The reason: there are so many tasks to be done when you're your own boss. Choosing the highest return option isn't always easy.

Doing What You're Good At

Business owners and solopreneurs generally gravitate to what they're good at doing. As such, they devote a lot of energy to their strengths and avoid their weaknesses.

On the one hand, this is smart—you're doing that which you excel at doing. On the other hand, you're allowing your weakness to cost you money. Not because you're lazy, but because you stick with your strength.

Ever go to the gym and see a guy who does bench presses his entire workout? His chest is big and he's really strong. Except for his legs. They look like toothpicks. The reason: He concentrates on his strength—bench presses.

This commonly happens when practitioners turn into business owners. The amazing bulldozer operator spends his days in the dozer seat because that's where he's comfortable. Only problem is, he's the owner of the company. He has a dozen mismanaged employees. Clients are peeved because their calls aren't returned. Multiple problems are festering while the owner is hard at work. Doing what he likes to do. Avoiding that which needs done.

A Tale of Two Bulldozer Operators

As a landowner, I've paid for a lot of excavating, originally, with an outfit resembling the preceding example: a hard worker, concentrating on what he's good at, while management of the business suffers.

Today, my go-to excavating company is owned by Jon, a former employee of the original company. He, too, runs a good dozer, but he focuses on running his business. I was one of Jon's first customers 11 years ago. At that time, he was scraping and scrapping to get established. Certainly, he was driven, but his clarity of purpose impressed me. "Damian," he said, "I want to be a business owner, not a bulldozer operator."

Jon's business is in growth mode because he doesn't hide on machinery, allowing problems to languish.

Look at yourself and your enterprise. Are you a bulldozer operator or a business owner?

Drive Means Working on Your Weaknesses

To achieve the life and business of your choosing requires drive. Drive equals discipline. We know you're ambitious. But are you disciplined enough to work on your weaknesses?

Success comes from exploiting your strengths. Longevity happens when you strengthen your weaknesses.

Most people are willing to work diligently doing something they love. It takes discipline to work at things you don't love and aren't good at. Driven business owners get through this knowing it's what's required to take them where they ultimately want to be.

Analyzing Your Work Habits

Where are you "busy" rather than productive?

_____

_____

_____

Recognize three areas of your business where you're working hard but could be more productive by working smarter.

_____

_____

_____

What work do you avoid because it is your weakness?

_____

_____

_____

The Talent Myth

I told you about my college roommate, Woody. Huge potential; not hugely prosperous.

Why? A lack of discipline. A lack of drive. A lack of deliberate practice.

What's deliberate practice, you ask? We'll get to that. First, a theorem I refer to as The Talent Myth.

> The Talent Myth: The misguided belief that success is based solely on natural talent.

Let's Talk About Talent

People have to live with themselves. That's why they tell themselves little lies. Lies comfort them. It's comforting to believe a lack of talent is holding them back from fame, fortune, or even middle class success. In telling themselves this lie, they never have to point the finger at themselves as the source of their mediocrity.

The Talent Myth perpetuates because it justifies one's lack of achievement. "I just wasn't born with talent," they say in consolation.

According to one author, they may be right.

In his book *Talent Is Overrated*, Geoff Colvin proclaims there is no such thing as natural talent. He asserts that all success is the result of years of deliberate practice. That is, rehearsing, training, and preparing, in a disciplined and methodical manner, to achieve a specific outcome.

I disagree with Mr. Colvin. I believe in talent because I started out in comedy. We all know the pain of watching an unfunny person attempt to deliver humor.

I believe in talent because I participated in sports. You likely did, too. Watch a sampling of people throw, catch, shoot, or kick a ball and natural talent is obvious.

Don't believe in talent? Go to karaoke night (if you enjoy pain!) for a display of musical talent or lack thereof. Stand a dozen different people at a chalkboard and ask them to draw you a picture.

Contrary to Mr. Colvin's assertion, there is a thing called natural talent. But, as previously stated, talent is just potential. Potential has no value until you apply the deliberate practice so acutely described by Mr. Colvin. When you combine potential *and* deliberate practice, the results are amazing.

We'll unearth and harness your talent in the chapter titled "Exploiting Your Talent Stack."

Lady Gaga and The Talent Myth

My niece was struck to discover I'm a Lady Gaga fan. This revelation came about during the singer's 2017 Super Bowl halftime performance.

While I can't claim membership in the Gaga fan club, I like her music. Although I'm more impressed with the singer's story. The woman is driven!

Stefanie Germanotta was playing the piano by age 4. At age 11 she was accepted into the prestigious Juilliard School but opted for a Catholic education instead. Gaga has been working with a voice coach, whose clients include Mick Jagger, since she was 13. She was admitted early into NYU's Tisch School of the Arts. She withdrew and worked as a go-go dancer, sang at New York clubs, and by age 20 was a song-writer at Interscope Records. Before you ever heard of Lady Gaga, she was penning music for the likes of Britney Spears and New Kids on the Block.

How many setbacks do you suppose young Stefanie endured in her drive to become Lady Gaga? Were her setbacks due to a lack of talent? Absolutely not.

After Lady Gaga jumped off the roof to open her Super Bowl halftime show in 2017, I explained the Lady Gaga backstory to my disappointed niece.

"I thought she was just naturally talented with a beautiful voice," my niece lamented. "This isn't nearly as impressive. It means that with enough work, you could be Lady Gaga."

Well, not exactly. Success requires talent *and* deliberate practice. I can work, but I can't sing. More importantly, if I wore a meat dress to an awards show, I'd eat it by intermission!

Talent is real. So, too, is The Talent Myth. You can delude yourself by saying you lack talent or you can capitalize on your potential through deliberate practice. Do the latter!

6 Resilience

At some point in your life's training you've probably heard this statement: "The hardest person to beat is the person who refuses to be beaten."

If you haven't heard that before now, your high school coach was an absolute letdown as a motivational speaker!

Joking aside, that statement is true. It's nearly impossible to beat someone who refuses to be beaten.

Resilience is the ability to readily recover from adversity or misfortune. We could use similar words like *willpower, fortitude,* and *perseverance* to describe traits of successful people. If success is your intention, become a person who refuses to be beaten.

There Will Be Bad Days

Your business, customers, employees, or the marketplace, will, at some point, beat the crap out of you. I'm not wishing this on you. I just know it'll happen. Because it happens to all of us endeavoring in our own enterprise.

There are always challenges and setbacks. Your success depends on your ability to shake off the setbacks and get back to work. It's permissible to remember your misfortune. In fact, you should learn from setbacks and use them as motivation. The beauty of weathering storms is that it teaches you you can weather the storm.

Rocky

There are several things to like about the movie *Rocky*. First off, it's a good story. Who doesn't pull for the underdog? Second, his training methods of chasing chickens and punching beef carcasses was cool. Third, and somehow this fact is lost on many people, Rocky got beat. Yep, in the original movie, Rocky was David to Apollo Creed's Goliath. Goliath won.

That's right, the hero lost. But Rocky earned the world's respect. Even though he lost, he went the distance with the world champion. The Italian Stallion proved he wasn't a chump.

The story of Rocky is a story of resilience. He refused to stay down. Even when his trainer, Mickey, advised him to do so, Rocky climbed to his feet and landed some good punches. Rocky went down swinging. It's hard to beat the person who refuses to be beaten.

Which brings me to this line that you should never forget:

> "It ain't about how hard you hit; it's about how hard you can GET HIT and keep moving forward."
>
> —Rocky Balboa

Your business will get hit. Mine has. I've put money into investments that became complete losses. Put out products that flopped. Had client relationships blow up. I endured months, even years, of professional and financial setbacks. And then there's just good, old-fashioned bad luck and bad timing. Imagine being in the business of political comedy right after the terrorist attacks of 9/11.

Develop the fortitude—the mental and emotional strength—to get through adversity.

As Rocky would tell you: It ain't about how shiny your product is or how smart you were in school. Sometimes, it's simply how hard you can get hit and keep moving forward!

Michael Jordan

From a fictional athlete now to a real one. A real good one, in fact. Michael Jordan, formerly of the Chicago Bulls.

The highlight reel on Mr. Jordan is a mile long. Probably longer. The man could play basketball. Twenty years after his retirement, they're still comparing him to Lebron James to determine who's the best of all time.

What stands out to me about Michael Jordan was one particular game against the Utah Jazz. It was Game 5 of the 1997 NBA finals. Sometimes called the "Flu Game," because Jordan was ill. Very ill. There are conspiracy theories that he really wasn't ill. Or that he was hung over. Or that it was all a con. I saw the game. I don't believe Jordan's a good enough actor to act that sick, despite his credits in *Space Jam*.

The nonconspiracy theory is that Jordan had food poisoning, not the flu. He was ill, dehydrated, exhausted, and about to pass out. Yet he still put up 38 points, seven rebounds, five assists, three steals, and one blocked shot.

The takeaway isn't that MJ was a great athlete. We know that. It's that he had this amazing accomplishment when he was deathly ill. That's resilience. With a good bit of fortitude and willpower mixed in.

Fewer than 500 men in the world play basketball in the NBA. Out of 7.5 billion people, fewer than 500. They are the best 500 players in the world. You'd think the difference between the number-one player and the 500th-best player would be almost undetectable. Yet, that's not the case.

Furthermore, wouldn't it stand to reason that the best player playing while deathly ill wouldn't be nearly as good as the other guys on the floor? So what separated Michael Jordan from the other amazing athletes? Willpower. Resilience. Fortitude. He refused to be beaten. By other players or even by food poisoning.

Can You Learn Resilience?

Later in this book, we'll discuss habits. You can learn habits. Traits, on the other hand, require a bit more work because they're part of who you are. Traits relate to your personality.

Of the four traits of success we cover, resilience is perhaps the most difficult to cultivate. Why is this so? Because risk tolerance can be logically dealt with. If you put risk in perspective, you realize your endeavor isn't as rife with peril as you initially imagined. Also, as I pointed out, risk exists everywhere.

When we talked about drive, I told you there's no such thing as an ambition gene. Drive is simply discipline. You can make yourself driven by making yourself go to work.

But can you make yourself resilient? Maybe, and that's enough reason to try.

Resilience is mental toughness. Resilience is pain tolerance. As Rocky said, how hard can you get hit and keep moving forward? Most people don't like getting hit!

Resilience is a personality trait that allows you to overcome misfortune. The interesting part: you exhibit resilience only by experiencing misfortune. While adversity weeds out the weak, it strengthens the resilient.

How You Can Strengthen Your Resolve

I want you to be a businessperson who refuses to be beaten. Here are some methods to help you bolster your mental toughness.

Remember Your Why

I get through adversity by reminding myself of why I'm doing what I do. In the next chapter, we're going to find your "why," meaning, what is the purpose that caused you to start on this journey to begin with?

Being my own boss, in charge of my earnings, using my creativity—those were my "whys" when I started this endeavor. Two decades in, I will not be denied those things. Remembering this strengthens my fortitude. It'll do the same for you.

Remember Your Adversity

Michael Jordan was cut from the varsity basketball squad as a high school sophomore. He never forgot. Tom Brady, the most successful quarterback in the history of the NFL was a sixth-round draft pick. One hundred ninety eight players were drafted before Mr. Brady. He didn't even start for his college football team until his senior year. Would you say Mr. Brady has used those setbacks to make himself stronger?

Don't like sports? Let's use Abraham Lincoln as an example. Abe's business went bankrupt. Abe was defeated in multiple elections. Abe then became one of the greatest presidents in

American history. Imagine how things might have ended up for America had we not had such a resilient man in office during the Civil War.

Never forget your misfortunes. When you know what you've been through, you know what you can get through.

Tell Yourself a Story

You can talk yourself into greater resolve. I developed a "you won't beat me" mentality because I believed I was underestimated. I told myself high school wrestling competitors underestimated me during weigh-ins. My competitors were weightlifter types; I was a rangy farm boy. They may or may not have underestimated me but it made me more determined to beat them if I thought so.

When I started in comedy, I was told by professional peers and bosses that I'd come crawling back for a job. It didn't happen. Every time the chips were down, I told myself that story. Believing I was underestimated by co-workers gave me fortitude.

There's real science behind this concept. I just read an article about successful entrepreneurs. It was once thought entrepreneurs ventured out on their own because they couldn't get along in a normal job environment. The reality: many entrepreneurs start and succeed with their own business because they felt undervalued by the workplace.

Entrepreneurs know their value is greater than they're being offered or paid. An example would be immigrants who lack a stellar resume to get a good job. So, they start a restaurant. They know they have more value than the marketplace realizes.

Being underestimated, undervalued, or even insulted does wonders for one's determination!

Are you underestimated?

The Wrap on Resilience

Resilience is your "bounce back factor;" your "I won't stay down" quotient; the part of you that absolutely will not be denied.

While you can't change your personality very much, you can increase your mental toughness. This requires discipline. A willingness to tolerate a certain amount of pain. A conscious mind-shift to perseverance when the former you would have surrendered.

Want to succeed in creating a life and business by choice? Be a person who refuses to be beaten.

What will you do to make yourself more resilient?

_____

_____

_____

Refuse to Stay Down

I met Ron after a speech for the National Pork Producers Council. Ron is an Iowa hog farmer. If your mental image is a guy in bib overalls clutching a squealing piglet, your image is inaccurate.

Modern agriculture is a business. Ron is a businessman. He owns hundreds of thousands of hogs. So many pigs that he contracts with other farmers to raise them

(continued)

(*continued*)

for him. Ron also owns and operates millions of dollars' worth of cropland.

We met at a meeting in Florida. He then brought me to Iowa for another pork industry event. That's where I got to know a good man with a great story.

To clarify, this is no inherited riches tale. Ron is self-made. All in the past 30 years, too. Because, like so many people in agriculture, he got washed out in the 1980s.

A Quick History Lesson

The 1980s farm bust was to agriculture what the stock market collapse of 1929 was to Wall Street. Probably worse. A result of plummeting land values, 18% interest rates, global commodity turmoil, and low prices. It was an awful time. I know because I lived through it. For perspective, some land was so upside down, the bank wouldn't even repossess it.

Ron lost everything. His farm ground; his hog barns; and his machinery. He was able to retain four acres and his family's home. At rock bottom, he and his wife borrowed money from her parents to buy groceries. Ron took a job as a UPS driver. Vowing he'd come back to the business he knew and loved—farming. Did he ever!

Never Lose Your Vision

Today, Ron is proud to say he paid off every creditor. That's impressive given how tumultuous the scene was three decades ago. His happiest day came when he was able to quit UPS to go full tilt back into agriculture.

He made one decision during his time in the brown uniform: He was going "wide open" to create the agricultural enterprise he knew he was capable of building.

This story could be about any person in any business. Ron never lost sight of what he wanted to do or what business he wanted to be in. He was willing to do whatever necessary to get through the struggle. Then, it was time to pull the trigger on the restart. He did so and never looked back.

Failure is a tremendous motivator. Failure is more educational than success. Failure is only fatal if you allow it to be.

7 Vision

The Farm

The farm where Lori and I live was an absolute showplace. The place had imagery straight out of a painting: cattle grazing in beautiful, rolling pastures outlined by painted board fences. Immaculate landscaping. Pretty, historic barns. A stately, old, professionally decorated house. You'd call the place a country manor.

The only problem: The picture I just described is how the farm looked in the 1970s. We bought the property in 2006!

The place had been vacant for a decade. The decade before its vacancy, the elderly owners were failing. The barns, house, and grounds had deteriorated from neglect. The house was livable—the heirs had left the utilities on—but extremely dated and in need of extensive renovation. Same for the barns and the grounds. Even the crop fields required a lot of TLC.

I was raised a few miles from the property. I remembered it in its grandeur. My wife didn't. The first time she saw the place, she said no. The second time we looked at it, the vision began to click. We saw past the cobwebs, as they say. Our cobwebs were dilapidated buildings, drainage issues, and all manner of infrastructure.

A couple years, a couple hundred thousand dollars of renovations, and thousands of hours of manual labor later, we had a show farm again.

I told you this story because visualizing what something can become, versus what it currently is, is vision. Most people cannot do this.

Partners with Vision

My wife and I live and work together. We run my business, manage the farms, and oversee a few other things. One strength we possess is vision. We can both look at a pile of turds and see the (eventual) Taj Mahal.

Vision is a tremendous strength as a married couple. Shared vision is paramount to a successful business partnership. If you're partnered with someone who can't see the end result of what you are building, dissolve the partnership!

When I quit my job to strike out on my own, I had a vision for what I wanted to build. At the time, I was dating a law student. I explained my vision for the long term and where I saw myself going. She scoffed. We broke up. Clearly, we were not compatible on vision.

What Vision Is

Vision means the power of anticipating that which will or may come to be.

Vision, like the three previous traits we've covered, is a trait of successful people. It's largely innate but just like the three previous traits, you can enhance your vision.

When you look at the future, what do you see? What does this mean for your business? Where are the opportunities? Where do you face extinction? What must you do to prosper in the next decade? Where do you see yourself? How observant of the world around you, are you?

Those questions, and the answers you provide to those questions, define how much of a visionary you are.

Your Purple Wall

We live in a world in which most people can't look past the color of a wall. Have you watched those home renovation programs? HGTV is my wife's favorite channel, so forgive me for all the real estate examples. Seriously though, have you watched these hapless home shoppers who can't get past the color of a wall? You're gonna tear the damn wall down anyway! Who cares if it's purple?

Again, that's vision. Can you imagine missing out on a solid investment because you couldn't see past a purple wall? A gallon of good paint costs $30. Look past the purple.

I will submit that I'm color-blind. This may actually benefit my vision because I don't get hung up on meaningless little things like paint color.

You need to be color-blind too, metaphorically speaking. Learn to look past little objections and keep your eye on the prize. That's vision.

I see this all the time with businesspeople who aren't as successful as they could be. They can't see beyond a short-term obstacle—call it their purple wall. The end result is what matters. What's currently in front of you doesn't.

It's not what you start with; it's what you end up with. Focus on the end result. That's vision.

Why You Need Vision

Why do you need vision and why is it a success trait?

1. Without vision, you miss out on opportunities that your vision-less peers left on the table.
2. The vision you possess for yourself and your creation will provide direction during stormy weather.
3. Vision is where you are headed. It's the outcome(s) you desire. The end you envision is what drove you to begin in the first place!

The Big Picture. Most People Don't See It!

Vision is a success trait because it's in very short supply.

Vision comes from two things: Aspiration you have for yourself and paying attention to the world.

A visionary is a person who:

1. Sees what others can't.
2. Looks beyond the immediate.
3. Observes everything, knowing future opportunities arise for those with a worldview.

A Tale of Two Dairymen

We rent our farmland to a young, progressive dairy farmer. He moved to the United States from the Netherlands as a 13-year-old, graduated from Michigan State University, and became an American citizen last year.

Johan understands the big picture. He has vision for where his operation is going. He contemplates opportunities, looking past short-term obstacles. He knows milk is sold in a global marketplace. He monitors movements in New Zealand and dairy industry changes in California as those things impact the marketplace.

On the other hand, there's Bob. Bob hasn't moved from the farm he was raised on. He works hard. But he doesn't read much. His worldview is limited. He's struggling now.

Bob blames "mega dairies" like Johan's for putting him out of business. He seeks out people who agree with him on that opinion. But what opportunities did Bob leave on the table because he lacks vision? What changes in the marketplace did Bob not see coming because he worked every day with blinders on?

Vision means looking ahead and seeing your business profitably occupying a space in the future. Vision does *not* mean you have every decision made for the rest of your life. That's impossible. Foolish, even. There are too many variables.

Many people—the very people you'll be more successful than—are stuck with a horizon the size of their backyard. Possess a worldview.

The Big Picture: A Lesson from Comedy

Comedy is a difficult business. Breaking into the business is tough; building a successful career even tougher.

You've heard of open mic nights? Great example of how difficult the business is.

Aspiring comics show up on Tuesday night and work for free. Sometimes they even pay for stage time to hone their craft.

Ever hear of "open accountant night"? Of course you haven't, because there's no such thing. Can you imagine bean counters working for free every Tuesday night to hone their skill at calculating tax returns?

I've been an open-miker. It's painful. The biggest problem for some open mic night performers is limited material. I don't mean limited like they have only five minutes. I mean limited in its appeal. This points to a lack of vision.

One night I particularly recall, a guy was doing decent material that had absolutely no potential. Not because it wasn't funny, but because it had no scope.

His comedy set centered on the Arizona Diamondbacks' struggles in that year's playoffs. He had 10 minutes of material citing names and places. You see the problem here? Who, outside of metro Phoenix, gives a damn? Answer: No one.

You can't build an act with national appeal if your focus is your backyard. Another problem: those jokes have a short shelf life. Want more mass appeal and timelessness? Make jokes about the Cleveland Browns' struggles. They're perennially bad and everyone laughs at Cleveland.

Vision means you understand the big picture. Look at the big picture. Now look at your business.

Is your offering too limited geographically or demographically?

How can you increase its appeal?

What steps can you take to make your product less time sensitive?

How can you grow your business with clientele outside of your backyard?

How to Improve Your Vision

If a visionary is someone who sees what others don't, most people by definition aren't visionaries. There are degrees, of course.

Let's look at automobiles, for example. Preston Tucker was a visionary. He invented a car ahead of its time and was then targeted by Detroit's Big Three automakers. Before Tucker, there was Henry Ford. Ford was a visionary. Current day, Tesla's Elon Musk is either a visionary or a con man. I'm not sure yet which.

You needn't be Preston Tucker, Henry Ford, or Elon Musk to be classified as a visionary. You simply have to pay attention.

I used comedy to explain Big Picture thinking for a reason. You know what's integrally important to a career being professionally funny? Observing.

That's it. Just paying attention. Make note of trends in the marketplace. Read a variety of books and publications. Observe your fellow human beings. Put down your phone and look around.

Going deeper, pay attention to the emotion of the moment. If you sense everyone in the marketplace is nervous and selling, that's a good time to buy. Conversely, if you observe an irrational amount of exuberance in the marketplace (think dot-com bubble), it's time to sell.

Have you ever heard the old advice, "the time to walk is when everyone is running and the time to run is when everyone else is walking"? There is truth to that. It doesn't make you a brilliant visionary; it makes you smart enough to observe, then go against the grain. Humans struggle with going against the grain. Herd mentality is real.

Sometimes vision means willingness to go against the grain when you see what the herd doesn't. You can profit from the herd by seeing what they don't!

Just Because Your Neighbor
Is Doing It . . .

In 2006, my wife and I rented a home in Arizona for the winter. Every week I looked at real estate. But I knew it was the wrong time to purchase. The marketplace had simply gone up too much too fast.

At that time, an Arizona State economics professor was quoted in the local paper saying, "There are no fundamental problems with the Arizona real estate market."

I sensed otherwise. I traveled every week to other states for work. I saw how out of whack Florida, Nevada, California, and Arizona real estate were compared to other states. Being a political comedian taught me to read a variety of sources. Not only to glean different perspectives for comedy, but also to be better rounded.

I wasn't about to take the gospel of an Arizona State professor, quoted in *The Arizona Republic*, talking about Arizona real estate, to Arizona readers who desperately wanted to believe they were smart for overpaying for their Arizona homes.

You've heard of preaching to the choir? Well, sometimes the choir loves the sermon so much they don't realize the preacher is bamboozling them. When I toured open houses, real estate agents told me, "Better buy this house. These places are increasing in price 30% every year."

Lori and I didn't buy an Arizona property in 2006. But we did in 2009 after the market tanked. We paid half what the house had sold for three years earlier. You know, back when "these places are increasing over 30% per year."

The following year we purchased a foreclosed property for less than one third of its previous price. By then, the real estate bust was in its third year and people were running scared. Which meant it was a good time to buy.

Sometimes vision is simply paying attention, taking a big-picture view, and a willingness to go against the herd. Remember the thing about following the herd: only the boss cow has a clear view; the rest are staring at another bovine's butt!

Your Big Picture

People love to talk about dreams. "It's my dream to . . ." fill in the blank here. It's right up there with "I just want to be happy!" You've already heard my stance on that dumbass statement of responsibility dodging.

One problem with dreams is that they're dreams. In my dreams, I'm James Bond or back on the high school football field. In my dreams, I'm bigger, stronger, and faster than I was as a teenager. I know it's a dream because my knees don't hurt.

Don't tell me your dreams, tell me your vision.

We'll clarify your vision by asking two questions:

1. Why are you embarking on your business endeavor?
2. What do you want your life and business to look like?

The first question will motivate you to fulfill your personal vision.

The second question is the big picture you see for yourself. You couldn't possibly answer it with one word or one sentence. That's okay.

My Why

Before you get overwhelmed contemplating your why, I'll give you mine. It came to me in 1994. I was an unhappy, yet successful, lighting fixture sales rep. It was time to make a change. Various business concepts were explored. From landscape lighting, to bar ownership, to flipping fixer-uppers.

The only problem: I had no money. I was 25, paying off college debt, and renting the fourth-floor loft of my buddy's condo.

Regardless, it was time for a change. So, I spent a little time in contemplation. Notice I said, "a little"? Most people get stuck here because of fear. It took me less than a month to make a decision. I asked a simple question: Why do I want to be in business for myself?

The answer: to be compensated based on my effort and to be creative.

What I Want My Life and Business to Look Like

Again, I'll go first. Then you need to answer those two questions.

I know with absolute clarity what I want my life to look like and it boils down to three words: Wealth, Fulfillment, and Location.

- **Wealth:** Not for the sake of bragging, but for the independence of choice it allows. It's why I've worked since age 8 and saved my money. As wealth builds, I can increasingly say, "No" to unappealing work or deals I don't like.

- **Fulfillment:** Because we all know people who have money with no purpose. Days filled with accomplishment and enrichment make for nights filled with contented sleep.
- **Location:** Where you live matters. Correction, where you live may not matter, but where I live sure as hell matters! My life vision doesn't have me residing in Barrow, Alaska.

Now It's Your Turn

You'll save yourself a lot of frustration by clarifying your vision early on.

Why are you starting/running your own business?

_____

_____

_____

What do you want your life to look like?

_____

_____

_____

2

Habits

8 Success Is a Habit, But It's Not a Routine

We usually think of habits as negative. Smoking rather than flossing, for example. Habits are like peer pressure in that regard. But peer pressure is only bad if your peers are bad.

Peer pressure can be quite positive. I have peers who challenge me to achieve more, read more, work smarter, think differently, and squeeze more out of life. A lot of unproductive, unhappy people would do well to find positive peers to pressure them!

So it is with habits. They can be good or bad. Success comes from cultivating good habits.

Habit versus Routine

There's a difference between habit and routine. One is intentional, the other mindless. No matter what your picture of success looks like, you won't get there by being mindless.

A couple of definitions for clarity:

> *Habit:* an acquired behavior pattern regularly followed until it has become almost involuntary.

Routine: regular, unvarying, habitual, unimaginative, or rote procedure.

"But Damian," you're saying, "the word habitual is in the definition of routine." Yep, it is. Along with unvarying and unimaginative. Are those adjectives you'd like to see on your tombstone?

Also the word rote is used to describe routine. Rote means "without thought."

Unimaginatively and unvaryingly plodding through life without thought never yields positive results.

As an aside, that last sentence made me think of one of my favorite movie lines from *Animal House*:

"Fat, drunk, and stupid is no way to go through life, son."— Dean Wormer, Faber College.

Habit, as opposed to routine, is defined as an acquired behavior pattern. See the difference? Acquired is active. That means you sought it out and made it happen. Intentionally.

Cumulative Effects of Habits

Good or bad, habits don't generally make you or break you immediately. Unless you're talking about a serious drug habit, which can be quickly lethal.

Habits have a cumulative effect. They're like compound interest in that regard. The physically fit person isn't fit because she exercised Tuesday. She's fit because she exercises every Tuesday. Several other days of the week, too. So it goes with building wealth, growing your business, getting smarter, and everything else in life.

Create positive, intentional actions, do them habitually, and the benefits pile up over time.

The Daily Sale Habit

My friend and insurance agent has a policy about insurance policies: He won't quit for the day until he's sold one.

That was the advice given by his grandfather, who started the agency. Tom cultivated it into a habit. Intentionally. He demands of himself that he sell at least one new insurance policy per day.

That's disciplined and deliberate. After three decades of daily habit, the cumulative effect is a prosperous business.

Make Yourself Uncomfortable!

Humans fall into routines quite easily because routines are comfortable. Routines don't vary. Most people are okay with not varying. Variation means change and humans don't do change well. Change is uncomfortable. Which is why you absolutely must make yourself uncomfortable.

In the chapters that follow, I provide you 10 habits of success. Initiating new habits is uncomfortable. We're talking about actively altering what you do and how you do it. The results will amaze you.

Comfort is the enemy. With comfort comes complacency. And thinking that sounds like this: "That's how we've always done it." Creativity doesn't come from being comfortable.

Here are simple methods to make yourself uncomfortable.

- Move where you work.
- Change your daily schedule—you'll be amazed at the new perspective you have just by varying your day.

- Exercise. If you already are an exerciser, change what exercises you do.
- Implement two new activities into every day.
- Read something you don't normally read. Start by just reading; period. Most people don't read at all.

When you make yourself uncomfortable, you think differently. Thinking differently is good for business.

Examining Your Habits

On a scale of 1—10, rate your business habits

_____

On a scale of 1—10 rate your personal habits

_____

What activities do you regularly and intentionally do that are positive for your business?

_____
_____
_____
_____
_____

What bad habits should you eliminate to be more successful?

_____
_____
_____

What routines will you change to make yourself uncomfortable?

_____
_____
_____

The Success Habits

We've established that habits are active, conscious, behaviors. Habits are intentional, unlike routines, which are done without thought.

Want to do business better? Start by developing these habits of success. Here are the chapters to take you there:

1. Pull the Trigger
2. Treat Time Like Money
3. Be a Goal Setter
4. Be Relevant
5. Be Critical
6. Be a Promoter
7. Sell, Sell, Sell!
8. Know Your Position
9. Stop Making Excuses
10. Know Money (Or You'll Have No Money)

Creating the life and business of one's choosing requires one to first make an active choice. Make the choice to develop good habits.

9 Pull the Trigger

ots of people struggle with making decisions. Usually, it's not for a lack of information. It most often boils down to fear. Fear of the unknown, fear of judgment, fear of taking responsibility, and the biggie—fear of change.

So, these fear-based operators plod along in a state of perpetual undecidedness. They tell themselves and anyone who'll listen, they're "thinking about making a change."

Guess what? It never happens. Ever. They just can't pull the trigger.

Paralysis by Analysis

We all know people suffering from paralysis by analysis. They're not really overwhelmed with too much data—it's their emotions that have them paralyzed.

When they say, "I just don't know what to do!" What they're really saying is, "I'm terrified of decisions and change. So, I'll pretend it's more complex than it really is."

I don't want you to be this person. And to clarify, it's almost never more complex than it appears.

Here, then, is your guide to effectively executing decisions.

- **Enough Is Enough:** At some point, you've gathered all the information you need. Beyond that, you're just looking for excuses.
- **Advice:** Seek out someone with more knowledge than you, who has successfully navigated a situation similar to yours. Offer to pay that person for guidance. Remember, with advice, you get what you pay for!
- **Impose a Deadline:** When people don't *have* to do something, they typically don't. Firm deadlines, with consequences, create decisiveness.

No Decision *Is* a Decision

Have you heard the old business statement, "No Decision *is* a Decision"? After enough time passes, the person afraid to choose, has made a choice. By default.

Then comes the justification. Because nobody wants to admit they've deferred every time life gave them choices. Much easier to pretend their life was a purposeful journey. Even though it wasn't.

Is this what you want? Decision by default, then justify the result? I didn't think so.

Life and business require daily choices. Be a person who firmly executes decisions. The empowerment you feel will outweigh the worry associated with the choice.

Incidentally, most of what you're worrying about isn't going to happen. So stop festering over the "what ifs" and pull the trigger.

Admit it, you don't respect your wishy-washy peers. You admire decisive folks. So, become one.

Decisions, Decisions

What decisions are you postponing?

_____

_____

_____

I'm not going to ask you why you're postponing the decision. It doesn't matter. For each above decision write down what you'll do to gain information or advice.

_____

_____

_____

Now give yourself a _realistic_ deadline on those decisions. Lots of nondecision makers are "going to decide in a few years." And they never do! When will you pull the trigger?

_____

_____

_____

10 Treat Time Like Money

An entrepreneur friend of mine relayed something he'd heard at a business roundtable: "Everyone uses 100% of their time."

Simple as that sounds, it's pretty provocative. Because the logical followup is, "doing what?"

Ask anyone, and they'll tell you they're busy. But busy doing what, exactly? Building the life and business of their choosing? Or filling their calendar with unproductive, yet self-imposed, commitments? Making themselves better? Or numbing themselves with mindless passivity?

525,600 Minutes

Each of us has 525,600 minutes each year. Except for leap year, when you get an additional 1,440 minutes, this number doesn't change. Doesn't change for me, you, the rich, the poor, the uneducated, or the person with a PhD.

We all get the same number of minutes. How you commit those minutes correlates directly to your success and happiness.

Time Is Money

In business, we commonly hear the saying, "Time is money." If that's true, you'd think people would be more discerning with their hours. Sadly, most people mismanage both their money and their time.

According to the U.S. Census Bureau, median household income (half earned more, half earned less) in 2017 was $61,400. Median income per person in the United States in 2017 was $31,786. That's $15.89 per hour on a 2,000-hour work year, or just about 26 cents per minute.

What are your minutes worth? Run the math. Now look at your daily routine.

If your time was actual cash, would you spend it the way you're spending your time?

Remember, routines are mindless and without thought. By analyzing your time critically, you're likely to find a lot of mindless activity that's not a wise investment of your valuable time.

By the way, don't count sleep hours. Your waking minutes decrease in value if you're not rested—ya gotta sleep!

Downtime versus Wasting Time

You're saying, "Damian, you can't work every minute of your life. A person needs downtime!"

Agreed. But there's a difference between downtime and wasting time. For example: In 2016, the average American adult watched five hours and four minutes of TV per day. Using the median hourly rate, would you pay $80 every day to watch television?

The Five E's

To maximize productivity while maintaining a balanced life, I apportion time into the five E's. This is helpful because it forces me to categorize my hours and my activity. These are my categories. Yours may differ based on what you value.

The important step is that you mindfully analyze how you spend your time. Look at your week and see how much time fits into each of the five E's.

- **Enterprise:** This is your career or business. Even if you love it, it's still work. Don't let it consume every waking moment!
- **Exercise:** Movement of body sharpens the mind and feeds the soul.
- **Enrichment and Education:** You know that feeling you get when you learn something new? Increase those positive moments in your life by investing time learning and enriching yourself. Read, join a club, take a class. Make time to make yourself better.
- **Enjoyment:** Success without joy is like a convertible in Siberia—what's the point? Family, hobbies, and stimulating conversation with friends is time well spent.

It's Your Time

I created the five E's for me. If I can't slot my hours or minutes doing an activity into one of those categories, I eliminate said activity. Likewise, too much time spent on one "E" is cause for a rebalance.

Evaluating Your E's

Using the five E's template, what are your categories?

_____

_____

Where do you spend your time?

_____

_____

Where can you admit to yourself that you are wasting time?

_____

_____

We're occasionally asked, "What is your time worth?" Maybe it's from an outside service company pitching their ability to make your life easier by saving you time. But we really should be asking ourselves this question every day.

You have 1,440 daily minutes to invest. What are they worth and how will you invest them?

The $5,000 Fallacy and Four More Hours

During my junior year in college, I took a personal finance class. This wasn't the most studious era of my life. Which means I was forced to _retake_ the class! Taking personal finance twice was one of the best things that ever happened to me.

One lesson I particularly remember from that class was the $5,000 fallacy. Granted, this was a long time ago. Five grand may not seem like much today. The concept is the same regardless of the dollar amount.

In a study conducted by a financial organization, a vast majority of people stated they'd save and invest more money if their earnings increased by $5,000. The remarkable thing: $5,000 was the consistent number, regardless of income. High earners in excess of six figures and those with incomes of $20,000 agreed, they'd commit more to savings if they earned just $5,000 more each year.

The point: most people spend every dime they make. Regardless of how many dimes they make.

Guess what? It's the same story when it comes to time.

Give Me Four More Hours

When interviewing businesspeople on my podcast, I ask: "If I gave you four more hours per week, how would you spend those hours?"

People never struggle to answer how they'd spend additional time. What they're really saying when they answer the four-hour question is: "I don't do as much of "X" as I should. I know it's important. But it's not so important to me that I'm doing it now."

Remind you of the $5,000 Fallacy? People know they should save. But saving isn't as important to them as frivolous expenditures. So they pretend they'll more responsibly invest the next $5,000.

(continued)

(*continued*)

I can't magically give you four more hours. You already have them. Just like most folks have money they could save and invest. They just choose not to, then make excuses for why they aren't.

I'll ask again: How would you spend four extra hours per week if you had them?

Now where are you going to find those four hours in your existing week?

You can always tell yourself you don't have enough time or money. Or that you'll do a better job managing it when you get more of it. That's a fallacy.

Make yourself rich by investing the time and money you already have.

11 Be a Goal Setter

told you up front I've never had a formal business plan. Never. I've also never penned a corporate mission statement. But from day one, I've had goals.

For fun, I went to the website of the Small Business Administration. It came up after Googling "business plan." SBA is a federal agency with 3,300 employees and a $710 million budget. Their website states: "A business plan is an essential road map for business success. This living document generally projects three to five years ahead and outlines the route a company intends to take to grow revenues."

How many of those 3,300 government employees have started, owned, or run their own business, do you suppose? I'm guessing none.

I'm not discounting the importance of having a plan. I'm discounting the importance of formal business plans.

A more practical tool in your quest to do business better is goal setting.

The Problem with Business Plans

A business plan is an instruction manual to run your business for the next five-plus years. How the hell would you know that when you're just starting out?

Here's the problem with a business plan as it's defined:

- The marketplace is in constant motion. An "essential road map" as SBA calls it is useless when the landscape and roads all change.
- A business plan becomes antiquated quickly. What you planned to do isn't working. But you discovered a way to make tons of money selling widgets that weren't even invented when you drafted your business plan. What do you do? Keep chugging with your 20-page "essential road map" or make money instead?
- Bankers love business plans. That should be your first warning to avoid them! Bankers don't do change. ATMs and the drive-up window were revolutionary advancements for them. In short, a formal business plan is required to borrow money; it's not required to make money.
- Some aspiring entrepreneurs spend so much time crafting their theoretical plan they fall in love with it. They commit to it like a religious doctrine. Then they won't vary from the plan. You need flexibility, not rigidity to succeed. New opportunities present themselves.

> You need a formal business plan to borrow money, not to make money!

Mission Statements Are Even Worse

I worked in corporate. Maybe you did, too. Do you remember your company's mission statement? Did it drive your daily activity? Was it clear in stating what you'd accomplish and where you'd end up? The things you need to do this year to be more successful?

Here's a mission statement I pulled off a company website. This happens to be for a grocery chain, but it could be any large organization.

Guided by relentless focus on our five imperatives, we will constantly strive to implement the critical initiatives required to achieve our vision. In doing this, we will deliver operational excellence in every corner of the Company and meet or exceed our commitments to the many constituencies we serve. All of our long-term strategies and short-term actions will be molded by a set of core values that are shared by each and every associate.

What the hell does that even mean? Five imperatives? What are the critical initiatives and who's implementing them?

Mission Statement Equals Corporate Poetry

I'm all for motivating and guiding employees. That's what mission statements are supposed to do. Reread the preceding gibberish. Now tell me what the kid bagging groceries is supposed to do because of it. In general, mission statements are corporate poetry.

Just Do It!

I saw an interview with Phil Knight, the founder of Nike. He was discussing his book, *Shoe Dog*. To say Mr. Knight has done well as a businessman is quite an understatement. His net worth is estimated at $35 billion. Why am I telling you this? Because Phil Knight says he never had a formal business plan for Nike.

Success is about doing. Not talking about doing. Which is what most formal business plans and mission statements end up being—just talk.

Humans love to procrastinate under the guise of "planning." They plan, contemplate, research, deliberate, then ultimately decide, "This wasn't the right opportunity." Or, "The timing just wasn't right." Or, "We're not sure the marketplace will support this endeavor."

News flash: There's never a perfect time, right economy, or golden opportunity. That's why I advocate for a more action-oriented approach than drafting a 20-page document.

Goals: What Are They?

Goals focus your objective and guide daily activity. Goals specify the vision you have for yourself and your business. Goals are specific results you want to achieve with a *deadline*.

The deadline is critically important.

Why You Need to Set Goals

The big answer, of course, is to be successful and happy. Beyond that, here's why you must set them.

- We all have a tendency toward distractions. Goals keep you focused on important stuff and filter it from the insignificant.
- Goals set a vision for the short term, medium term, and long term.
- Goals provide clarity and accountability. You said you'd do this; it's documented; now get it done.
- Goals are quantifiable. Wordy mission statements the HR department took six months to craft over a dozen

committee reviews are not! "Sell a million dollars of product in the next three years" is measurable.

- Goals are flexible. I set mine annually and I review them. The marketplace evolves, so must you to achieve your vision.

Goals versus Shopping List

I once explained the value of goal setting to one of my sisters. She loved the idea. She committed herself to disciplined goal setting. A year later, she told me about the things she had bought that were on her goal list.

We all like stuff. I have toys, too. By all means, reward yourself for your accomplishment. A goal to pay off your car loans early and purchase real estate is a goal. But when your goal sheet looks like a Neiman Marcus catalog, you're missing the big picture.

Goals versus New Year's Resolutions

I set my goals every year at Christmas time. It's a reflective time to look back at the year that was. What did you do right? What didn't you accomplish that you said you would? What will you accomplish in the New Year?

When recapping the prior year, I give myself a letter grade. Did I earn what I said I'd earn and invest the amount I set as my investment goal? Did I correct the personal failings I seek to improve? Did I write a new book like I said I would? Then, next to that line item I write in marker, A+, B–, C+ . . . and sometimes even an F!

You gave yourself an "F?" Yes. Every small businessperson focuses on one goal at the expense of another. Letter grades crystallize which items you need to work on for next year's goals.

Even though I do this at Christmas time, you should do yours whenever it makes sense for you. The main thing is that you commit yourself to setting and achieving goals. Don't confuse goals with New Year's resolutions. Resolutions are January First wishes with a champagne toast.

Very few positive changes come about from resolutions uttered after three plates of meatballs and several toasts to the New Year.

How to Set Goals

I set goals under three umbrellas: Personal, Financial, and Business. You can start with the same three categories since most everything fits into one of those columns.

Categorization isn't the priority, achievement is. The old saying "the proof is in the pudding" comes to mind here—you can say you're a goal setter but results are all that matter.

- **Personal:** What do you want to accomplish this year in your personal life? Enhance your relationship with your children? Spend more quality time with your spouse or partner? Write it down. Under that entry put three actions you *will* take to make it a reality.
- **Financial:** In your financial section, document what exactly you want to attain and how you will do it. Want $100,000 of savings and investments in five years? Write it down. Now what will you do to make that happen? Complete an online personal finance class? Pare back spending on discretionary items by $600 per month?
- **Business:** The business section is always the lengthiest of my goal sheet. Yours probably will be, too. Document your objectives and actions you will take to get there.

Your goal is to Do Business Better. Are you going to complete training to make you a better businessperson? Revamp your customer base? If so, how many new customers will you have by the year's end? What about the end of next year? How much revenue will your enterprise gross? How much of revenue will you commit to marketing and new product development?

Your Goal Sheet

You've seen the examples. Now let's do your goal sheet.

Personal

1. _____
2. _____
3. _____

Financial

1. _____
2. _____
3. _____

Business

1. _____
2. _____
3. _____

Vision: Your Fourth Category

We talked about the trait of vision up front. Goals help you crystallize your vision. As you set your goals, ask yourself:

- What do you want your life and enterprise to look like?
- What do you want your financial picture to look like? (Use real numbers here!)
- What do you want your daily activity to look like?
- Relationships?
- Where do you want to live?

Your Goals Are Set. Now What?

Look at them a few times per week to keep yourself motivated. You need reminders of where you're going. Your goals sheet is a "To-Do" list to the life and business of your choosing.

I keep a printed copy in my desk and a digital document on my computer. I encourage you to do the same. Distractions are everpresent. Goals keep you focused on where you're going.

Saying, "I just want to be happy" isn't tangible. When you make goal setting *and* goal attainment a routine part of your life and business, you'll know what makes you happy.

12 Be Relevant

Staying relevant is more than just a habit of success; it's a critical necessity of success. Travelers checks lost relevance. The Yellow Pages lost relevance. Video rental stores lost relevance. Are you getting the point?

Losing relevance is the first step toward business demise. I preach to clients on the need to reinvent. Why? Because you have no choice. The marketplace evolves. You either adapt or perish. Harsh though it may be, I didn't make the rules. The marketplace did (and does!).

If you adapt, you survive. If you go beyond mere adapting, reinvent yourself and your business, you do better than merely surviving; you'll thrive.

Relevance Equals Demand

Since we all work for other people, the only way to thrive is to remain relevant in the eyes of those we serve. This goes for solopreneurs, little companies, huge companies, and even entire industries.

Relevance means a segment of the marketplace needs you in their life. Your business does better when your product makes someone's life or business better.

The Relevance Reality

Customers pay for what matters to them. When you no longer matter, your demand fades. Next, you're irrelevant. After that, you're out of business.

Your job, in addition to your job, is to remain relevant to the marketplace. This is a constant challenge because the marketplace is in constant motion.

Changing Marketplace

Generally, technology is the force behind change. Pay phones, for example, are no longer relevant to me. Most other people, too, for that matter. Twenty years ago I couldn't run my business without pay phones. Do you remember long-distance calling cards? Rows of pay phones lining the walls of airports? When's the last time you saw payphones getting used? Or even saw a pay phone?

Printed road maps fall into the same category. They're less relevant now because of technology.

The list is a mile long of items and industries supplanted by technology.

Unless you worked as a pay phone repairman or sold maps for a living, you haven't been negatively impacted by these changes. Which brings up these questions: Will you, your profession, or your industry lose relevance? How long until you'll lose demand? Maybe even become unnecessary?

No one likes to think about the demise of their business. The thought of your own obsolescence is uncomfortable, to say the least.

We all resist change to a certain degree. But change is coming whether we like it or not. A good success habit is to regularly analyze what you offer. Then ask yourself, "What must I do to remain professionally viable?"

Let's look at residential real estate sales as a case study. This in no way is to pick on real estate agents, it's simply an illustration. Look at yourself and your business and ask:

> Are you about to become irrelevant like Realtors are?

Again, this is a business lesson, not a personal attack. I have several friends and a sister who are real estate agents. Believe me, I want you to succeed. To do so, you're gonna have to change. Fast!

Technology Comes Home

My wife and I have bought and sold numerous pieces of real estate. On the recent sale of an investment property, we went Realtor-less. It worked great.

Real estate websites like Zillow are not yet transactional venues. You can shop, snoop, and look at pictures, but for the most part, you don't click and purchase a home. Yet. Remember, no one bought groceries or books online a few years ago, either.

Enter FSBO Tech

Lori and I engaged the services of a company called FSBO Tech. For an initial fee of $159, you get access to required legal documents, professional photography, and listings on real estate sites and the multilisting service.

The property sold in less than two weeks. An additional fee of $400 was collected by FSBO Tech at closing. $559 beats the heck out of the standard seller commission of 6%. This is why Realtors, as we know them, will soon be extinct.

When You See Realtors, Do You See You?

Each of us faces the threat of professional extinction. The Realtor's competition isn't other Realtors, it's an evolving marketplace. Think of Yellow Cab, who thought their competition was another cab company only to find out it's Uber.

Technology is changing—and cheapening—real estate transactions just as it changed and cheapened ground transportation. Is this happening to your industry?

Know What You Sell

Before you can reinvent to remain relevant, you must first clearly understand what you're in the business of providing.

Real estate agents would likely say their clients pay them to value their homes. Or handle the transaction. Or verify a home's condition. Or negotiate the deal.

In actuality, Realtors don't do three of those things and the fourth is debatable.

The value is set by the marketplace, calculated by appraisers, and approved by the lender. Title companies complete and record the transaction. Licensed inspectors verify the property's condition.

The Reality of Realtor Negotiations

Realtors would likely tout their value in negotiating on their client's behalf. The data doesn't back this up. The book

Freakonomics, by Steven Levitt and Stephen J. Dubner, devotes an entire chapter to why Realtors aren't really negotiating for you.

As you keep hearing me say, customers pay for what matters to them. In a similar vein, humans are motivated by their own interest. Even if they happen to be working for you as your Realtor.

The usual arrangement when two Realtors are involved—a buyer's and a seller's—is to split the 6%. Then the agent has a split with her broker. Leaving, typically, 1.5% of the sale price as their take.

Which means every $10,000 of sale or purchase price is $9,400 to you, and only $150 to your agent. If you're a buyer and you overpay by 20 grand for a property, that's an additional $300 of income to your agent. Why would the agent stop you from overpaying? If you are a seller with a median American home worth $275,000, your agent might encourage you to take an offer of 20 grand less than asking price. The agent sacrifices $300 in commission but still makes $ 4,125.

> Your real estate agent's real priority is finding more clients!

Bringing It Home

Most home sellers and buyers' biggest need is fear mitigation. They want someone to shepherd them through an unfamiliar experience. Hence, a real estate agent's biggest value is soothing anxious clients. But for how much longer will that be necessary?

A decade ago, nobody bought cars online. Five years ago nobody hopped in a stranger's car for a ride dialed up on a smartphone app. Technology made these two formerly scary activities—riding with a stranger and shopping for a car—less scary. Home buying and selling is next.

How Realtors Can Reposition For Success

Whether you're a Realtor or a widget maker, the objective is to remain professionally viable. You want to be in demand in tomorrow's marketplace. Ideally, demand for your product or service increases. To make that happen, you must evolve.

Here are four options for real estate agent reinvention. As you read them, think of your own business. What do you need to do to stay in demand in the future?

Be an (Amazing) Expert Know stuff that Zillow doesn't. Your clients have Google Maps. They don't need you to tell them this house is close to the freeway. Know everything about schools, nearby service providers, and neighborhood history. Instead of selling homes, make your product knowledge.

Do It All Take your service to the next level. Make everything turnkey. Not just a phone number for the moving company you recommend—turnkey! Meaning you manage and oversee everything for your client. Moving is stressful. Transferring utilities, coordinating packers, lining up cleaners, and four dozen other tasks come along with moving. When you remove customer's stress, you're compensated.

In a world where people pay to have their dog walked, there is money to be made in added service. Consider yourself a real estate concierge.

Renovation Most homes require work. Do it. Vertically integrate your business and boost your revenue by alleviating the headache of remodeling. Most Realtors sell a house and say,

"It just needs a little TLC." Then they hand over the keys and head down the road. There the client sits with a home in need of renovation, and no clue how to make it happen.

The majority of home shoppers can't envision a wall being removed or shutters being replaced. They not only can't do the work, they can't even imagine what it will look like. A renovating real estate agent can improve her client's asset value. When you make your client's money, you make money!

Money Speaking of money . . . the Internet makes everything cheaper and transparent. Remember how daunting it used to be to book a trip? Pretty simple now, isn't it? That's why there are less than half the number of travel agents than there were in the year 2000. By the time you're reading this, travel agents will be even less prevalent. Maybe even extinct.

Online home sites will have a similar effect on real estate agents.

Realtors can remain viable by eliminating commissions and charging a flat fee. Tomorrow's real estate agent is a real estate consultant and advisor. Think flat-fee financial advisors. Instead of advising on stocks and CDs, you're advising on property assets.

Online home sites won't completely eliminate the physical act of looking at homes. As my Realtor friend likes to say, "You can't smell the cat urine in the carpet over the Internet." True. But tomorrow's consumer won't pay 6% for a home tour to smell the carpet.

Bringing It Home

There is no conspiracy against Realtors or travel agents or your profession. It's simply the evolution of the marketplace. Technology WILL disrupt your industry.

A habit of success is looking ahead and proactively repositioning yourself in a changing environment. Here's how.

Assessing Your Relevance Risk

View yourself from your customer's perspective. What is your product or service? (Hint, it may not be what you think it is. Remember the Realtor example!)

Will technology make you unnecessary?

Can you utilize said technology to reposition yourself?

We outlined four routes for Realtors to reposition themselves. What four actions can you take to reposition yourself?

1. _____
2. _____
3. _____
4. _____

What changes in the marketplace are causing/will cause your demand to fade?

_____
_____
_____

What actions will you take to remain relevant?

_____
_____
_____

When it comes to your reinvention, remember these three things:

1. Relevance equals demand.
2. Demand increases based on the value you deliver.
3. Customers pay for what matters to them!

13   **Be Critical**

We live in an era of hypersensitivity. Political correctness runs rampant. Safe spaces are demanded on college campuses so the delicate young adults won't have to hear dissenting views. We are full tilt into a focus on feelings. Offending someone—and this is increasingly easy to do in a society of safe spaces—verges on a felony-level crime.

I bring this up because this chapter is apt to hurt some feelings. The advice here runs counter to a world gone touchy-feely. If you want to get better, you need to get over yourself.

This chapter is about the benefits of critical analysis. It's time to recognize your mistakes and missed opportunities. I'm advising you to be critical. Of yourself.

You Can't Handle the Truth!

"You can't handle the truth!" is a famous line from Jack Nicholson's character, Marine Colonel Nathan Jessup, in *A Few Good Men*. Colonel Jessup was right. Most people can't handle the truth. But you're not most people. You've read this far because you're on a quest to do business better. Fantastic. You'll do so by being straight with yourself. You need to be self-critical. Sure it'll be tough to hear but it will yield results.

I know, you're not supposed to be self-critical. You're supposed to surround yourself with glowing people who ride purple unicorns and pat you on the back telling you you're wonderful. We've been doing that in our schools and suburban soccer fields for 20 years. The result: a bunch of kids who think everyone is a winner.

I'm Not Exaggerating

We've been hearing about the soccer trophy thing for two decades. Some well-intentioned idiots decided a couple of decades ago they didn't want their team to feel like losers so they stopped keeping score. Then they awarded everyone trophies. No winners; no losers. At a certain age, that's fine. Who thinks four-year-olds should be in such structured environments anyway? Let them play! And no, they don't need trophies for playing.

The "Everyone Wins" Movement Goes to School

In 2016, 47% of high school students nationwide graduated with an "A." Are we really going to pretend there isn't a grade inflation problem in this country? Speaking of grade inflation, you know that old saying, "It's lonely at the top"? Not so when it comes to modern-day Valedictorianism. Washington-Lee High School in Arlington, Virginia, boasted 178 valedictorians in the class of 2016. That was one of every three graduates.

My favorite topic of discussion at high school grad-uations is to ask kids their GPA. An amazing number of them possess a number higher than 4.0 on a 4.0 scale. When I ask them how it's possible to achieve greater than a 4 on a 4 scale, they tell me it's due to honors classes. Then I ask, "What's the maximum a GPA could be?" They always tell me it's 4. Even though they have a 4.23. Apparently, it's infinity.

Not Everyone Is a Winner

If you want to win in life and business, you gotta get better. Believe it or not, you're not amazing at everything. There are things you've never even done. How could you be amazing at these things? I know, this logical concept flies in the face of modern society.

Soon, those Valedictorians with shelves of soccer trophies will discover they aren't as amazing as they've been told.

I predict huge profit potential for therapists treating "Post-Valedictorian Unearned Trophy Syndrome."

Now then, back to your business. If you suck, you fail. There are no social promotions. So you have to constantly improve how you do what you do. You do that by critically analyzing what you do and how you do it.

Breaking Down Tape

A big part of my earnings are derived from speaking at corpo-rate and association events. I didn't major in public speaking in college. My degree is in Agricultural Economics. I've completed one speech class in my life. I think I got a "B."

So how does one get better at talking in front of audiences? First off, talk in front of lots of audiences. That gives experience. However, if you really want to ramp up the learning curve, break down tape.

Okay, that's an old term. We don't use video- or audiotape anymore; it's all digital. I still refer to it as "breaking down tape" because it takes me back to my formative years.

How to Break Down Tape

I'm going to tell you how to do this from the perspective of a professional presenter. The fundamentals are the same for you and your business. The objective is to improve your product by looking at it critically and methodically.

You're saying, "Criticism is mean, Damian!"

I didn't say be insulting. I didn't say pick on the poor kids on the playground. I said be critical. And methodical. Of yourself! It is truly the only way to get better. Comedians do it; football teams do it; and you should do it. Here's how.

Do It Immediately There's a reason football teams watch game film the day or two after their game. The game is still fresh in their memories. The time for improving on what you do is immediately after you just did it.

When you complete a sales call or finish a big project for a client, immediately "break down tape." Analyze what went right and what went wrong during the interaction? How will you improve for the next time?

Do It Regularly Viewing yourself from the third-person perspective is powerful. But not if you only do it once. Make it a regular habit to analyze yourself, your business, and your client interactions. Always ask yourself, "What could I have done better?"

Take Notes When I sit down to roll tape, I have a notepad. I write down what illustrations resonated and what jokes hit or didn't hit. Documenting your observations on paper makes it more likely you'll actually improve upon what you're analyzing.

Feel the Room A benefit of analyzing your actions after the fact, from an observer's standpoint, is the ability to sense client emotion. Now that you're not "in the moment," pull back and perceive the situation from the client's emotional state. Remember, people make decisions based on emotion, then rationalize it with logic after the fact.

Tighten the Act Watch yourself in action and ask: Where are you wasting time that doesn't accomplish anything for the client? In comedy, it's called tightening the act. Seinfeld calls it efficiency. I refer to it as compressing. We're taking a four-minute bit with five laughs and cutting out the fat to retain the five laughs but doing so with a two-minute bit.

How can you get the same result for your business (the laughs) with less input (words/stage time)?

Cut Material When analyzing a speech or comedy show, you get better by cutting material from the program. Maybe it's outdated. Or perhaps it was something new you tried multiple times and it just doesn't resonate with the crowd.

Look at your business. What product is it time to cut? What's getting stale? What experimental offering just isn't resonating with the marketplace?

Breaking Down Tape for Your Business

Take a recent client experience. Replay the tape in your head. View yourself as an outside observer.

Ask yourself these questions:

- What do you see?
- What notes would you jot down to improve the process for the next time?
- Now that you're away from the situation, could you alter your emotional state to better connect with the client?
- Where in your interactions and processes could you "tighten your act" to be more efficient?
- What "material" is it time to cut? What is outdated or not performing?

After you do this once, make it a regular habit!

The *Big* Benefit of Breaking Down Tape

We get so caught up in what we're doing, we forget we are doing it for our customers. That's why I did the comparison to show biz and speaking. A paramount rule I never forget: Without a paying audience, there's no need for me!

Same deal for your business, too, isn't it? Never lose sight of the fact you exist because of a paying client base.

Which brings me to the BIG benefit of methodical self-critique: It forces you to view yourself from your customer's perspective rather than your own.

A rule of business I preach:

Think Like Your Customers, Not Like Yourself

Take a critical look at what you provide your paying clientele. From their angle, ask yourself:

- **What are they seeing?** *You* might think it's no big deal that your truck is in disrepair and looks like it just completed a demolition derby, but what does the customer see? Inventory in disarray, uninterested employees playing on their phones, unkempt offices . . . What are your clients observing?
- **What are they feeling?** My wife and I just had lunch at one of our favorite little spots. The owner was feuding with her kid in the kitchen. It was noisy. Awkward, even. We'll eat there less often now. The vibe you and your employees give off does *not* go unnoticed!
- **What matters to them?** You think you know what clients value but until you see through their eyes, you don't. There's very likely a disconnect. Left unchecked, you'll lose the client because they don't think you understand or care about them.

Need more motivation on why you should think like your customers, not like yourself. I'll modify an old Earl Nightingale quote:

> Every dollar you'll earn the rest of your life is someone else's dollar right now.

We all work for other people. Pull yourself back, look at your business from their perspective and you shall prosper!

14 Be a Promoter

If you're an advertising executive, feel free to correct me. But for the purposes of helping you do business better, I'll define marketing, advertising, and sales from my small-business perspective.

Marketing is telling the world what you do.

Advertising is telling a specific segment of the world what you can do for them.

Sales is asking that specific segment of the world for the order.

We'll talk about sales in a later chapter. Here we'll discuss building your brand through advertising and marketing effort.

Advertising 101

I took an advertising class in college. I distinctly recall a rule of advertising as it was taught in the old days: Don't ever spend money on a marketing effort unless you can track the results.

That sounds reasonable, doesn't it? Advertising costs money. Therefore, be cautious about the investment you're making and monitor the returns. The problem: How do you do that, exactly?

You could possibly measure returns by experimenting with just one new marketing concept for a month and tracking sales.

Except sales volume might dip or spike during the same time you're experimenting. Seasonality, a competitor's adjustment, or any of a dozen other reasons could play a bigger role than your marketing trial.

Your experimental marketing move might look like a huge success if sales double while you're doing it. Until you find out the new activity had nothing to do with your billboard. Your competitor ran out of widgets and you were the only place with widget inventory. Hence, the sales bump.

I'm not advising you to avoid new marketing and advertising ventures. I invest heavily (percentagewise) in branding, marketing, advertising, and outreach. Which is why I know firsthand how difficult it is to scientifically gauge one marketing action's return on investment.

I have lots of hooks in the water at any given time. Who can accurately say whether or not this one action was the reason revenue was up or down? My business has a seasonal component to it. Much as I'd like to blame or commend one marketing experiment, the time of year matters, too.

Again, yes, spend money on marketing. Do so carefully. Don't make the mistake of thinking you can precisely attribute results to any specific campaign. Here's why it's gotten more difficult.

How Many Media?

Another problem with that old rule of advertising arises with the shear number of media. How many different places could you put effort into paid promotion? A hundred years ago there were basically three: print media, word of mouth, and signage. Then came radio. Then TV. Then the Internet. And on it goes.

Just four decades ago, when I was a kid, there were but three TV networks. Now how many channels are there? The same goes for radio. There used to be a few stations on the AM dial.

Then came FM. Now there's satellite radio. Print? It's still here, although newspapers are dwindling or going online. Along with blogs, vlogs, podcasts, a dozen or so social media formats, websites, and more.

We still have billboards, and they're getting fancier. Even small towns look like Times Square with electronic outdoor ads.

And you're going to track the results from every dollar spent on promotion across all these media? Good luck with that.

Do What Works for You

It sounds simplistic, but you have to do the marketing and advertising that works for you. The important thing is that you do it, period. The world doesn't know who you are, what you do, or what you can do for them.

Consistency and Methods

One rule of marketing I subscribe to: vary your methods but not your frequency.

Presenting your message through different methods keeps you from looking stagnant in the marketplace. Also, your consumer may be evolving. What worked yesterday—say, an ad in the Yellow Pages, doesn't penetrate anymore. Now it's targeted advertising on social media.

Business Is Good; Why Advertise?

It's tempting when times are good to say, "I don't need to advertise."

That's a bad idea but the mindset prevails in a lot of small business circles. I've even heard businessowners scoff at their competition saying, "If they have to advertise, they must be hurting." That's a backward way of looking at things. I'll give you some numbers from my beloved Coca-Cola for perspective.

In 2017, Coke spent $4 billion worldwide on branding initiatives. That's 11% of the company's revenue. A couple questions to help you up your promotional prowess.

Are you spending 11% of your revenue on branding initiatives?

Are you better known or less known than Coke? I can answer this one for you!

If one of the most recognizable brands on the planet invests 11% of revenue on marketing, why wouldn't it be reasonable for you to do the same?

What percentage of revenue are you devoting to your promotional effort?

Equally backward as the "We don't have to advertise because we're not slow" crowd are businesspeople who say, "We can't afford to advertise because business is bad." Oh, my.

These people need to start looking at some ads for their next step: As in, "Help Wanted" ads.

Your Branding Goal

Your branding goal is to avoid commoditization. When customers perceive no difference between you and anyone else in the marketplace, you're now competing on price. You can't win long term by being cheaper. There's always some dum-dum willing to give away his product for almost free.

There are three levels of attainment in the branding of your company or product:

1. Brand awareness
2. Brand preference
3. And the hardest to attain, brand insistence

Let's go back to Coca-Cola, for example. Almost every human on earth is aware of Coke. Some customers prefer Coke over other drinks and prefer it to Pepsi. Then there are consumers like me who *insist* on Coca-Cola Classic. I even avoid restaurants unless they serve Classic Coke.

You want your brand to be known. You like your brand to be preferred. Your objective is brand insistence!

Sporting Clays and Your Marketplace

To achieve brand awareness, preference, or insistence, your effort must hit prospects where they are, not where they've been. To illustrate what I mean, I'll introduce you to an activity I enjoy called sporting clays.

In sporting clays, you're attempting to hit a flying clay target with pellets fired from a shotgun. It's sometimes referred to as "golf with a shotgun." Except in golf, the greens don't move.

Similar to golf, you travel around a course and shoot from different stations. Some targets are moving slow, some fast. Some are high, some are low. Some travel right to left; others, left to right. Some targets are moving away while others travel directly toward you.

For a business example, imagine the sporting clays course as the marketplace. Clay targets—those four-inch flying discs—are customers and prospects.

The more targets you break, the higher your score. Kind of the same thing with your business, isn't it? Every customer is in motion. Yet, almost none of them are on the same trajectory.

The Shotgun Approach

There's an old reference, less used today because of firearm sensitivity, about the shotgun versus rifle approach. A shotgun shoots dozens of little pellets. A rifle fires a single projectile.

The shotgun approach is usually deemed bad because of its lack of focus. The rifle approach, conversely, focuses narrowly on the target. Focus sounds good. The shotgun approach is scattered. Scattered sounds bad.

But there's a problem with the rifle approach. It only works if your target is stationary. Are your customers sitting still? What about the marketplace? Is it sitting still? Of course not. Customers and the marketplace are changing as rapidly as ever.

Your Business

So there's your business on the sporting clays course known as the marketplace. Targets are flying everywhere. You opt for the shotgun approach, knowing dozens of pellets are better than a single projectile. Your pellets are every effort you exert to grow your business: phone calls, direct mail, website, Facebook, Twitter, LinkedIn, Instagram, Snapchat, sales calls, consulting meetings, trade shows, television ads, podcast interviews, radio spots, print media, promotional incentives, blogs, YouTube videos, email, civic club involvement, public relations, and professional association membership.

A long list, isn't it? What are your pellets? List every action you take to grow business.

Most pellets will completely miss your target. The good news? It only takes a couple of pellets to break a target. And the two pellets that were successful this shot won't be next time. That's why you need lots of pellets!

Shoot Where the Target Is Going, Not Where It's Been

In sporting clays, you fail if you aim where the target is. To succeed, you pull the trigger while pointing at bare air several feet in front of the target. Because that's where the target will be when your pellets arrive. The same goes for the marketplace. Put the pellets of your effort where customers will be, not where they've been.

15 Sell, Sell, Sell!

There's an old saying among peddlers: "If nobody sells, a terrible thing happens: nothing."

You may or may not like the idea of being a salesperson. Doesn't matter. If you're in business, in any capacity, the above statement holds. Without sales, nothing happens. You can't pay the light bill, let alone the talent you hope to employ to make your business thrive, without sales.

My former employer, Cooper Lighting, now a subsidiary of Eaton Corporation, was fond of saying, "We're a sales-driven company."

Aren't they all? Yes, we were in the business of manufacturing light fixtures, but the factories wouldn't run without orders from customers. Those orders came in through the sales department.

Without sales, you have no business.

Sales Equals Revenue

Government raises revenue by taking it from its citizens through taxes. If you don't pay, you face prosecution. In business, we don't have that power. We must sell some good or service to create our revenue.

Your objective is to do business better. A key component of that goal can be attained by selling your company's offerings better.

A Few Things I've Learned About Sales

I've sold Cutco knives, herbicide, oil absorbent products, light fixtures, and Ag products. I've taken sales classes and participated in sales training. More educational than all that: lessons from selling the services of my own business since 1994.

A few things:

- Sales skills are teachable. Individuals who say they're not "natural born" salespeople follow that statement with "I'm just not comfortable asking people to buy." Guess what, you're in business now. You know what is a hell of a lot more uncomfortable than asking someone to buy? Losing your business and bankrupting your family. That's what.
- No matter how fantastic your idea, product, or service is, it will never get liftoff without a deliberate sales effort. You know that thing they told you about building a better mousetrap and the world will beat a path to your door? That's bullshit. There are plenty of mediocre mousetraps making money for their designers and manufacturers.
- Speaking of your brilliant, amazing, never before seen, revolutionary mousetrap... If your concept is bold, new, and different, you'll need 10 times the salesmanship to make it a success. The world resists bold, new, and different. Remember, human beings attacked the first hot air balloon with pitchforks thinking it was the devil. "Bold and brilliant" requires greater sales effort than "tried and true."

Are you ready for a crash course in professional selling?

What Selling Is

Some people freak out over selling. They think it's trickery, fast talking, bamboozling of unsuspecting clients. I'm convinced these people have watched *Used Cars* one too many times. If you've not seen *Used Cars*, order it up some night. Just for Kurt Russell's wardrobe. *Used Cars* too dated for you? Try *The Wolf of Wall Street* for unscrupulous salesmanship. You needn't be pushy to successfully sell.

My wife is a lovely woman with many talents. Sales isn't one of them. Or at least it didn't used to be. She was the epitome of the old salesman crack, "You couldn't sell Band-Aids at a train wreck."

Then Lori went back to work in corporate. In sales! After her first couple of months she'd had absolutely no sales training. Then she gave me a huge compliment. "Damian," she said, "everything I know about professional selling I learned from watching you run your business."

Feels good when your spouse sees value in what you do. That's when I told Lori this simple piece of sales wisdom:

> Sales, at its core, is understanding a person's problem and positioning yourself as the solution.

Ten Rules to Sales Success

Now that we've gotten you past your fear of sales, it's time to learn how to sell. Here are my 10 rules.

Rule 1: Have a Salable Product

First and foremost, have a salable product. The greatest salesperson on Earth struggles to sell something that has no purpose.

Calvin Coolidge?

Two years into my foray into political comedy I received a phone call. My act was starting to take off. The guy on the line explained that he'd been keeping up with my career. Told me he, too, wanted to have a successful political comedy act.

I asked the gentleman what exactly his act entailed. Mine, at the time, was a comedy show delivered in the persona of Bill Clinton. At that time, Bill Clinton was in the Oval Office. The guy on the phone told me he was a professional Calvin Coolidge impersonator.

I thought this was a crank call. But it wasn't. This guy wanted my help. This was a long-distance call back in the days when you still paid for long distance. The guy was serious. He sought my counsel on selling and marketing an act that had no relevance. Calvin Coolidge hadn't been in office for 70 years! He wasn't a funny president—Hell, he was barely even known anymore.

Want to be prosperous in sales? First, have a salable product.

Rule 2: Constantly Improve Your Product

It's not enough to have one good idea or produce one good product. Eventually, good isn't good enough. Apply daily effort to making your product better. And by "better" I mean more useful and more relevant to a paying customer.

Rule 3: Continuously Cultivate New Clients

Talk to any VP of sales and they'll tell you, this is where old salespeople stagnate. Sure, they still move product. They have a nice book of business. But they haven't reeled in a new prospect since the Reagan administration. Why? Because even good salespeople become complacent. Even seasoned salespeople get gun shy about banging on new doors.

Serve your current clientele. But never stop finding new customers. Past customers go away. Some of your clients change careers and you're now on the outs. Stay in business long enough and you'll have customers who die. Dead people can't buy your product. Tomorrow's success will very likely come from a relationship you haven't even started.

Rule 4: Listen

I told you up front but it bears repeating: Sales is understanding a person's problem and positioning yourself as the solution.

Notice I said, "person," not prospect or customer. Never forget that businesses serve people. Listen to them!

People will tell you what they need if you listen. If you're too busy yakking about yourself and your offering, you'll never hear their pain and miss out on being the remedy.

Rule 5: Don't Un-Sell Yourself

This happens all the time. Usually due to nervousness. Bad salespeople talk themselves out of a sale.

Be confident in yourself and your product. Ask your customer for their business. Then shut up.

Rule 6: Deliver

Nothing harms your reputation like taking a client's money and then not delivering what you said you would.

The Door Slammed Shut

My wife and I ordered a custom front door for a house we were renovating once. The sales guy was Johnny on the Spot when it came to selling his company's door. He gave us a lead time of four to six weeks. Three months later we still didn't have our door, but they had our money.

When it did show up, the installers were far from what you'd call "craftsmen." When you're buying a $6,000 door, there are certain expectations. Leaving your customer with a mess, a scratched door, and angry about a three-month wait is a surefire way to lose future sales.

Lori and I are renovating another property now. With eight doors that need to be replaced. Think we'll consider using that company? Not a chance!

Never sell what you cannot deliver.

Rule 7: Have Professional Marketing Materials

You're in business. So look like a business. Which means promotional materials, website, glossy pictures, videos, whatever.

Books do get judged by their covers. People do make decisions about you on first appearances. Hire a professional to make you look good in print, online, and everywhere else.

Rule 8: Ask for the Order

Some people just aren't comfortable asking for the order. Get over it. This is your blood, sweat, and tears. Your business is your baby. You have sacrificed and clawed to build your brand.

Now show pride in what you've created. Ask people to give you money in exchange for your offering.

Rule 9: Don't Lie

At some point tonight you need to fall asleep. Are you able to do that knowing you lied to make a sale?

Illuminating Lesson

I once had a regional manager tell me, "Damian, you have to lie, otherwise nobody will like you." Is that good training or what!? Not long after those words of wisdom, I found myself in the office of a woman 30 years my senior. She'd been a customer of my employer for more years than I'd been alive.

My company was selling an identical product to her competitor's for 10% less than she paid. Not because of volume discount or prepaid inventory crediting. My superiors who'd made this arrangement with her cross-town competition were simply screwing this established customer.

She called me on it and I told her the truth. Why? Because my character is worth more than some damn light fixtures!

We all work for money, but what's your integrity worth?

Rule 10: Follow Up

Sales manuals are chock-full of stats about how many exposures it takes before a prospect buys.

That's part of why you should follow up. The other reason? It's the responsible thing to do.

Want to know how easy following up is? Ask your prospect when they'd like to hear back from you on a proposal. Mark it on the calendar, then call or email just like they asked you to. In the meantime, print up a bunch of postcards with some cool photos or brand imagery on the front and write your prospect a handwritten note. It works.

See how easy that was? Ten simple practices that, done diligently, will make your business a selling machine.

Here's your bonus eleventh rule. It's so important, it's almost a commandment:

> A sale is only a sale if you get paid; otherwise, it's a gift!

Taking orders will make your business prosper but only if you get paid for those orders.

Now let's talk about objections—the customer's and yours.

The Price Is Right

The first, loudest, easiest, and most common objection is price. It rolls off people's tongues so easily it's almost a surprise when you don't hear a price objection.

Understand this: "It's too much" is the equivalent of "I'm too busy." It's merely a convenient excuse. A lot of times, it works.

The lazy sales method is to be cheaper. Watch any hack of a salesperson in action and they'll lead with price. If your only sales tactic is to be cheaper than the rest of the marketplace, fire yourself and replace yourself with a sale sheet!

Don't sell on price. Sell on value proposition. Make it your goal to be so good that the issue of price doesn't even arise.

But I'm an Idea Person!

I hear this from aspiring entrepreneurs all the time. "I don't want to be in sales, I'm an idea person!"

Great. Take your ideas down to the city park, sit on a park bench and talk to yourself about your wonderful ideas. You won't have to sell anything. You won't have that awkward feeling of asking customers for their business.

Just sit on that park bench and be an idea person. Get comfortable. Because if you won't sell your ideas for actual money, that park bench will become your bed.

Ideas are fantastic. I have lots of them. Every day. I write them down and put many of them into action. But ideas need to be turned into products that alleviate customer pain points. Then the idea that turned into a product needs to be sold.

Selling Equals Responsiveness

A lot of sales success boils down to simply being responsive and responsible. It doesn't take talent to return calls, show up for appointments, or listen to a prospect explain their need. Then it's as easy as responding.

Sales Wisdom

I worked in Erie, Pennsylvania, one summer for a crusty, likable fellow named Pete Fox. Pete and Jane were business owners of the self-made variety. One of Pete's favorite lines was:

"Selling's like shaving. Do it every day or you look like a bum!"

Admittedly, it's not politically correct to call people bums. Furthermore, lots of people wear facial hair these days. But I've always liked the line. It points to the need for making sales a daily habit.

Final Sales Pitch

Selling isn't about being a huckster or fast talker. It's not about snake oil and silver-tongued pitches. Sales at its very core is understanding a customer's problem and then positioning yourself as the solution.

> Remember, if nobody sells, a terrible thing happens. Nothing!

To help you with your sales effort, answer these questions:

- Does your product present salability issues? Remember Calvin Coolidge?
- What tweaks and changes will you do to improve your offering?
- What practices should you implement to constantly cultivate new clients?
- Are you listening to your customers? To what the marketplace is telling you?
- Have you been guilty of talking too much and un-selling yourself?

- Do you deliver on your promise? Can you improve on your deliverables? (This matters—remember, there's a door company in Arizona missing out on a lot of future business!)
- What do your marketing materials look like? Do they cast you in your best light? How old are they? Is it time to revitalize the look?
- Are you asking for the order? Are there prospects you could be doing business with but haven't asked?
- Have you ever lied to make a sale? Be honest. Now keep being honest. When you lie to make a sale you just put a price on your integrity.
- Are you following up on potential business? Could you be more creative in how you follow up to create more enthusiasm?

The Reluctant Salesman

Still convinced sales isn't your thing? Meet Roy Applequist. I met Roy several years ago when his company hired me to speak at their international sales meeting.

Roy started Great Plains Manufacturing in 1976. He began by meeting with 100 farmers. He listened as they told him of their unmet needs. Then, he built a prototype 30-foot folding grain drill (a machine that seeds grain) to the specifications farmers had requested.

With the prototype in place, it was time to make some sales. Roy was a reluctant salesman. Whatever your image of a salesperson's personality is, think the opposite. But Roy had a fledgling company. To make it prosper, he knew he had to sell.

(continued)

(*continued*)

Roy amused me with the story of his first sales call. He explained how he nervously met with a large machinery dealer. He demonstrated the benefits of his piece of equipment. Then he asked for the order. While driving home, Roy told me, he stopped at a pay phone to call his wife.

"Honey," he said, "I've got good news and bad news. The good news is I just sold four grain drills. The bad news is, I've only built one."

Roy's company immediately ramped up production. All together, 25 grain drills were sold in the first year. One hundred were sold the next year and sales doubled the year after that.

In 2016, Great Plains Manufacturing was sold to a multinational company for $430 million. Not bad for a reluctant salesman!

16 Know Your Position

One surefire method to failure is failing to comprehend where one stands in a business arrangement. Underestimate your offering and you'll be taken advantage of. Overestimate your value and you'll be shown the door.

Successful businesspeople always understand their position.

Chess

I don't play chess but I often see business compared to the game. I'm more of a checkers guy. I also like the old board game of strategic battle known as Stratego.

Whether we're talking chess, checkers, or Stratego, the point is simple: you win by understanding your position and moving strategically better than your opponent does.

Your lesser pieces will never be more powerful than the opposition's king. Understand that and move accordingly. Business success has similarities. You win by moving in accordance with your position of strength.

Getting Cocky

Some people overestimate their value or demand. You see this when poorly managed small businesses are in an up cycle. All of a sudden, they stop advertising. They needlessly agitate customers. We're in the chips, the cocky, yet shortsighted business manager believes. Then comes the downturn. They go from booming to begging. If only they'd understood their position and realized their high was a blip, not a forever reality.

This happens to employees and businesses alike. They simply overvalue themselves. They overestimate their position. Which brings me to Lee.

Lee

A friend of mine works for a privately held company. The company has done very well over the years. The six employees are generously compensated. The owner, admittedly, has been a bit absent the past decade. This happens to older business owners sometimes after they've hit the jackpot.

The owner decided to sell the company. The manager, we'll call Lee, was assigned the task of meeting with prospective buyers. The problem: Lee wasn't fully on board with how things were supposed to go, per the owner's vision.

Lee has been with the company 35 years. According to Lee, the company can't run without him. Lee wasn't bashful about communicating this to potential buyers. Lee also saw the sale as an opportunity to enrich himself. He made certain demands to the suitors. Those actions ultimately sabotaged the sale of the company.

Lee was confronted by the owner. That's when Lee explained—to the owner—"This company hasn't needed your input for a decade!" Lee was immediately fired. As he should have been. Probably sooner than he was.

One should always understand one's position.

What's Your Position?

I commonly hear businesspeople callously state what they will and will not do. I always wonder, "Are you truly in a position to make such demands?"

Likewise, job seekers with no experience and little work ethic state what they will and will not accept. How is this possible? Presumably someone is subsidizing these picky job seekers.

It's fine to be demanding *if* your position warrants your demands!

It's as simple as this: If you want the Walmart account, you probably aren't going to be in charge. They are. Because they possess tremendous market power. Conversely, if your brand is hugely demanded and you have your pick of customers, you're in the position of strength.

Being in a less powerful position doesn't mean you are in a less profitable position. It just means you don't call the shots. This is when knowing your position is critical. While you can't call

all the shots, your objective is to call the shots that matter. Seek pricing, terms, or conditions that keep your business moving forward. At some point, we all serve customers in a stronger position than ourselves.

Understanding One's Position Doesn't Mean Kissing Butt

I've never been good at sucking up. Politically motivated schmoozing disgusts me. That's one of the underlying reasons I departed corporate America. Who wants a "merit-based raise" based on their merit at kissing ass? Not me.

Yet, I always understood my position. I worked for Cooper Industries. They were my bosses. Any power I held was based on my expertise or experience.

When I resigned, the higher-ups were shocked. How could a 25-year-old kid walk away from all this, they wondered?

Here's the lesson from that: People in positions of long-held power routinely overestimate their position. They wrongly believe you can't live without them. It's the old adage about power going to one's head. They've surrounded themselves with "yes men" for decades. They've had their butt kissed so much, their cheeks are beginning to chafe. They're convinced the web they spin is bigger than it really is.

You turn these people on their head by walking away. By not needing them, they're forced to reanalyze their position. Nothing miffs the complacently powerful like not being needed.

The same principle applies to your business.

How to Improve Your Position

The surest way to never be beholden to those higher on the food chain is to save money. Money buys independence.

You also improve your position by being really good at what you do. Adding value to yourself through training and experience improves your position, too. But don't fool yourself into thinking because you produce a really nice widget that the world can't live without you. It can. This is where successful businesspeople always comprehend where they stand in the marketplace.

Being financially sound allows you to walk from business you don't want. Money buys you freedom to demand better arrangements—because if the deal doesn't go through, you're still fine.

We'll talk about money in another chapter. Now that you realize financial stewardship gives you freedom and power of position, you'll take that chapter more seriously!

George

I told you about Lee, who overestimated his position. Now I'm going to tell you about my friend George, who always understands his position.

George went back to school at age 30 to become a veterinarian. Remember that point in the last section about improving one's position by adding value to yourself? He did that. He didn't have to. He was comfortable beforehand. But he wanted to run his own vet clinic rather than work for a pharmaceutical company.

George ran a successful veterinarian practice for years. He'll tell you the stories about being up all night working in hog facilities. Or getting called out in the

(continued)

(continued)

wee hours of a weekend night to doctor sick cattle. He was a service provider who'd worked hard to cultivate a clientele. His position merited that he do those things.

It wasn't all peachy starting his own practice. He came to town as a newly minted veterinarian to work for the big veterinarian in town. George blossomed. His vision had always been to run his own business. That's when the power position came into play.

His employer wasn't just the big vet in town, he was also well known, and the president of a local bank. He informed George he wasn't allowed to start his own business. "You work for me," George was told.

George quit and started his own vet clinic. George had money saved, a work ethic, and he'd added tremendous value to himself. His position had improved.

At age 60 George sold his practice. On his terms. He also sold some real estate years before that. I will forever recall the story of that transaction. A local gentleman was interested in the real estate. The prospective buyer approached George and stated his intention to make an offer. George made a preemptive statement I now use when the situation is appropriate: "Perfect. Don't insult me or embarrass yourself with a low offer."

I think about that statement all the time in my dealings.

It's important to understand power, and it's powerful to understand your position.

Knowing Your Position

Are you guilty of underestimating or overestimating your position?

What proactive steps can you take to improve your business position?

_____

_____

_____

17 Stop Making Excuses

Everyone has a reason for why they're not doing business better. Problem is, they're not really reasons. They're excuses. Half of this book is about dispelling excuses.

> Success comes from actually doing something, not from making excuses for why you didn't do something.

Put simply, you can always find an excuse. Excuses let you sleep at night. It's not your fault. The dog ate your homework. You're a victim of the economy. You're in the wrong field. You didn't have enough notice.

On and on the excuses flow. Some are so outrageous, they're laughable. I have a brother who's been financially irresponsible his entire life. His excuse for being broke since the 1980s is the recession of 2008.

Successful people don't make excuses. When they occasionally do, they even admit they're doing it. "I know, I'm making an excuse . . . I haven't completed this project and it's because I've just lost focus."

At least that's an honest statement. Beats the heck out of the overly used "I'm so busy, blah blah blah."

Scarcity as an Excuse

Generally, people use scarcity when concocting their excuses. They pretend they're not more successful because they lack something. Time, money, education, assistance, and so the list of scarcity-derived excuses goes. It's easier to list a shortage of things preventing goal attainment, than to admit what's really lacking: effort.

Which brings me to my theory on excuses and what I call the Myth of Inadequate Resources.

The Myth of Inadequate Resources

Occasionally, Lori and I tune into a show on HGTV called *House Hunters*. The premise: join home shoppers as they select real estate.

In almost every episode the house hunter says, "Oh, this home would be great for entertaining. We just don't have the right space for entertaining in our current location." To which I call, BS!

The reason you don't "entertain" in your current house has nothing to do with the space. It has to do with you! You've never gotten off the couch, whipped up snacks, iced down drinks, and hosted a party. Don't blame your kitchen; blame yourself. You don't "entertain" at your current address because you're not entertaining!

House Hunters illustrates the Myth of Inadequate Resources.

> The Myth of Inadequate Resources: The delusion you're unable to accomplish something because you lack the proper tools.

Entertaining Space?

A storage room can be fun. All you need is a bag of chips, a cooler, a card table, and a little music playing (which you can find on the phone in your pocket), and you have the makings of "entertaining space." The hard part: You'll have to schedule a time, invite your friends over, and be a host.

You needn't spend hundreds of thousands of dollars on real estate upgrades to entertain. In fact, I want HGTV to hire me for a sequel show to *House Hunters*. Call it *House Hunter Debunker*. I'll follow up with people who bought their homes saying, "Now I can entertain" to see how regularly they're actually entertaining. My guess? Never.

If you've never had friends over to socialize—or never had friends, period, for that matter—it's not because of your basement.

Doing versus Saying

The Myth of Inadequate Resources is a lie people tell themselves. People don't want to admit they're lazy. So, they blame their situation on a lack of proper tools.

Inadequate resources isn't the real culprit, but it's comforting for people to delude themselves.

Don't believe me? Give people proper resources and they still don't use them. I'll illustrate with another home and garden example.

Right up there with "now we can entertain" is "outdoor space is very important to us." Many televised house shoppers purport their love of the great outdoors. Although the research says most don't often venture there.

A national home builder conducted a study. Their buyers, by a huge majority, claimed outdoor space was extremely important to their purchase decision. Ample play area for the kids, and an outdoor entertaining area for the adults, was a critical factor in their residential decision.

A year later the studiers analyzed the habits of those homebuyers—Who now resided in homes with adequate outdoor space they said they valued. They averaged, as a family, 17 minutes per week outdoors.

People *say* they'll do lots of things. Like entertain. Or spend time outdoors. Or play with their kids in the yard. The reality is they don't. Even when they have the proper resources.

Want Another Example?

From the *Wall Street Journal,* January 2018: In a survey of renter preferences across the United States, 82% of renters say an onsite fitness center is an important building amenity, with 55% saying they wouldn't rent in a property without one. Yet 42% of the respondents say they rarely or never use their fitness center.

Mind you, that's self-reporting. Had it been an academic study, the reality is likely far more than 42%. Probably closer to the entire 82% who say they value onsite workout facilities never actually use the gym.

Another Locker Room Story

My brother and sister-in-law own a fitness facility. It's nice. Big-league nice. Thousands of square feet of gleaming space stocked with exercise equipment, workout areas, and personal trainers who make patrons do the work.

What's the key to results for their clients? Not the equipment and the gleaming space. It's the accountability provided by personal trainers. Because exercise equipment, like every other tool, only works if you do.

To illustrate the Myth of Inadequate Resources, I present my brother-in-law. Rob began training clients years ago. He was poor back then. Before he owned a gleaming gym, his training tools were: the floor, the wall, stairs, the outdoors, and a towel.

Blame inadequate resources all you want but most people have access to a wall, a floor, a set of stairs, the outdoors, and a towel. Yet 67% of Americans are overweight or obese.

Speaking of Overweight

You'll never battle the scale if my friend Kari is cooking your meals. Kari's a terrible cook. That's not fair. She's not a terrible cook. She's a noncook. I'm not sure she's ever boiled water. But it's not for a lack of resources. For her wedding, she was given a couple of thousand dollars' worth of kitchen gear.

When she unwrapped a nice set of pots and pans, she proclaimed, "Now I can cook!" Nope. If you never turned on the stove with your hand-me-down pans, shiny cookware won't magically make you Emeril.

When I visit Kari we dine on Velveeta slices and crackers. The pans are still brand-new!

The Myth of Inadequate Resources

Most people won't make the effort, then blame a lack of resources. Give them the resources and they blame a lack of time. Because people seldom accept blame and it's uncomfortable to admit laziness. Now you know why the Myth of Inadequate Resources persists.

What have you not accomplished that you blame on inadequate resources?

_____

_____

What actions will you take to accomplish those things now that you know it's not a shortage of resources?

_____

_____

Successful people make the effort. Unsuccessful people make excuses.

18

Know Money (Or You'll Have No Money)

I routinely have conversations with people who want to start their own business. They're so excited as they describe their concepts. They're frothy with ideas and enthusiasm as the venture hatches inside their head.

I listen as the aspiring business owner describes his or her creation.

Then I ask two questions:

1. "Can you go six months without making any money?"
2. Are you prepared in the next 12 to 24 months to not only not earn any income but also plow saved money into your creation, if necessary?"

This is where I lose most of the theoretical entrepreneurs. They say, "No, but my idea is revolutionary. . . . Nobody is doing this." Or, "Didn't you hear my business concept? Don't you think it will work?"

It doesn't matter whether or not I think it will work or if the idea is revolutionary. Your idea might be the most amazing idea that's ever been conceived. Doubtful, but maybe. Whether it is or isn't an idea bordering on genius doesn't matter. What matters is this: How are *you* on the subject of money?

The Money Reality Check

Ideas and enthusiasm are the lifeblood of entrepreneurialism. The point isn't to squash a person's creativity or bash anyone for their enthusiasm. My point here is to clearly communicate the importance of a money mind.

Whether you are an employee considering a foray into entrepreneurialism or 20 years into running your own venture, money matters.

A big part of doing business better is managing money better. Starting or expanding your business requires investment. Investment of personal and real capital. Time, energy, creativity, thought, and money.

This chapter is about money. For you to be successful and for your business to achieve longevity, you must comprehend the principles of finance. Don't like talking money? Too bad. You're in business now and businesses exist to earn a profit.

You needn't possess an MBA in finance. If you know how to use a calculator, a credit card, a checkbook, and cash, and if you can draw two categories on a sheet of paper, you have all you need.

In fact, if you think financial success is easier for really smart people, let me tell you about my doctor friend. We'll call him Sam. He's very smart. Broke, too.

Sam's Story

Sam invited me to play racquetball one evening at his health club. He's a member of two health clubs. Sam said we'd play; then have beers afterward. Sam needed to discuss an item of personal business about which he sought my input.

"I've got a problem," he said as our beverages were delivered to the table.

"What's the problem?" I inquired.

"I don't have any money," Sam replied.

At the time, the good doctor was earning $330,000. He had nothing to show for it. Zero net worth. 98% of the doctor's takehome pay was obligated before he even touched it. Several car leases, mortgages on two residences, clothing, a dozen wristwatches, health club memberships, and several more lifestyle items were the culprit.

To clarify, Sam's income wasn't the problem. He was earning almost six times the average American household income. Then spent every penny of it. And then some!

We went through a lot of discussion and I jotted down some numbers. I gave him solid recommendations on getting ahead.

He didn't hear a word of it. Because my advice required sacrifice. The recommendations would require changes.

As I picked up the tab for beers, he said, "I think I have a solution."

"Really," I said. "I just gave you a half hour of solutions."

"Yeah, I don't think I'm going to do any of those things," he replied. "I think I'm going to lease a Prius. I think that would be more economical."

This guy was hemorrhaging cash, yet his answer is to lease a new hybrid vehicle. Not buy a used car, or drop health club memberships, or back off on the monthly wardrobe acquisitions. No, his answer was to pretend a couple dollars in gas each week would make him solvent.

To overspenders like Dr. Sam, the "solution" is always more consumption, never sacrifice.

Let's Talk About Money

Every day, you and I apply our talents and effort in the pursuit of earning income. We work for money. If we sacrifice so much time and toil in pursuit of dollars, isn't it prudent to do the easy work of managing those dollars?

In business, money changes hands between you and your clients. So, how is it you think you can succeed without comprehending finance?

You're saying, "There's more to life than money. . . . The best things in life are free, like time with friends or watching a beautiful sunset." True. I like walks with my dog and a pretty sky, too, but those things don't buy groceries. Life requires money.

Want to do business better? Learn the basics of finance.

It won't take much to be head of the class. In 2016, the news reported that 63% of Americans don't have adequate savings to handle a $500 emergency bill should it arise.

Did you hear that? Two thirds of America can't come up with 500 bucks in an emergency? That's pathetic. As of this writing, median household income is almost 60 grand per year. Two thirds of Americans don't have one tenth of one month's median income in savings.

According to CNBC, America surpassed $1 trillion of credit card debt in 2017. The average American at the time of this writing is carrying $6,375 of credit card debt.

Some credit card users like me pay off their statement each month. Meaning those who don't are way in the red. CNBC reports the average household with credit card debt is carrying a balance of $16,883.

You can blame a poor economy, low incomes, stagnant wage growth, or whatever you choose. The reality is that most people spend everything they earn. Don't be one of those people.

Start at Home

You can't have the life and business of your choosing until you get a handle on your personal finances. Take out a sheet of paper and at the top, write down all the ways you make money. In the middle section, record all the ways you spend money. (Or use Figure 18.1 to record this information.)

Revenue (Top Section)

How much do you currently earn? What is your household income? If you have a normal job, let's use the after-tax net income. If you are self-employed like me, it varies, but give an approximate number for your adjusted gross income.

Revenue

Job _____
Rent _____
Interest _____
Other _____

Expenses (Bottom Section)

Now just under the revenue, in the middle of the paper, document your expenses.

How much does your current existence cost you? Put every category down where your money goes. Don't know where your

INCOME STATEMENT

Revenue	$ Amount
Job	
2nd Job	
Business income	
Rental income	
Interest	
Dividends	
Settlements	
Royalties	
Other: _____	
Total Revenue:	
Expenses	
Rent / Mortgage	
Insurances	
Car Payment 1	
Car Payment 2	
Car Payment 3	
Living Expenses	
Utilities	
Property Taxes	
Debt Obligation	
Other: _____	
Other: _____	
Total Expenses:	
Total Revenue – Total Expenses = Net Income (or Loss):	

FIGURE 18.1 Create an income statement.

money goes? Given that you sacrifice effort and time every day to earning money, wouldn't you think you'd keep better track of where it goes?

Expenses

a. rent/mortgage _____

b. insurances _____

c. cars _____

d. living expenses—food, utilities, and so forth _____ _____

e. consumption items/discretionary spending (speedboat, vacations, entertainment) _____

f. debt obligation (credit cards, consumer debt repayment)
_____

Subtract the sum of all these expenses from your income (revenue).

Now you have a personal income statement.

Are you spending everything you earn? Worse yet, are you spending more than you earn? If you're still not sure, open your credit card statements. If there's a balance on your credit card that you've not paid off in 30 days, you're overspending.

If you are spending more than you earn or as much as you earn, here is your first assignment: Change that habit.

Balance Sheet

For the nonfinancially minded, a balance sheet sounds like an intimidating document. It's not. Take out a piece of paper and divide it either vertically or horizontally. On one side put the word "Assets" and on the other side "Liabilities." (See Figure 18.2.)

BALANCE SHEET

Assets	$ Amount
Cash & Cash Equivalents *(savings accounts...)*	
Investment Accounts *(stocks, bonds, mutual funds...)*	
Retirement Accounts *(401(k), IRA, pension...)*	
Property *(residence, rental property, vehicle...)*	
Other *(loans to friends/family, jewelry, collectibles...)*	
Total Assets:	
Liabilities	
Expenses currently due	
Short-Term Credit *(credit cards, loans from friends/family, home line of credit...)*	
Loans & Mortgages *(residence, rental property, vehicle, student loans, business loans...)*	
Unpaid Taxes	
Other *(commitment to donate...)*	
Total Liabilities:	
Total Assets – Total Liabilities = Net Worth:	

FIGURE 18.2 Determine your net worth.

For some of you, this is rudimentary. But in a nation as indebted and financially illiterate as ours, the basics need to be revisited.

We've already talked about your expenses. Let's assume your mortgage but in addition to that, list all debts you have other than mortgage. Those debts go in the liabilities column.

Assets Matter

Under the assets column, include everything you have that has value. Next to the asset, write its dollar amount. Bank accounts, stocks, bonds, real estate . . . anything that has value. Collectibles count but be honest about what the real value is. You're probably the only person who believes your *Beetle Bailey* collectible soda pop can collection is worth a million dollars.

If you are just starting your venture or expanding your business, answer these two questions:

1. How much are you prepared to lose?
2. How much is really required?

How Much Are You Prepared to Invest or Lose?

Look at your just-completed balance sheet. How much of that could go away without giving you an ulcer? If you go "all in" and it doesn't pan out, will you be living on the streets?

How Much Is Really Required?

Being realistic, how much capital outlay will your new venture cost? Separate your wants from your needs. You may want a mahogany desk or a personal chef in your office but you sure as hell don't need those things.

What are your initial costs, as well as additional costs over the next 12 months?

That's your number to worry about. Tally up what you need in the way of capital equipment, promotional budget, supplies, training, hired help, and any other necessity in the first year. Add 20% to that number for miscellaneous and unforeseen expenses and now you know how much money you need.

Yes, it's okay to assume you'll have revenue coming in from your new venture. But how long will it take before that happens?

John the Chiropractor

John finished chiropractic school and did all the necessary things one must do to call him- or herself "chiropractor." Then he rented space, bought the necessary equipment, and opened his doors to the public. On Monday, nobody came in for an appointment. On Tuesday, nobody came in for an appointment. On Wednesday, nobody came in for an appointment. Thursday afternoon, John still hadn't seen the first paying customer. He sat down on his exam table and bawled.

If you've been in business for yourself, you understand how challenging the early days can be. This is why you should be very cautious about revenue expectations or projections in your first year.

I started my business with contracts totaling $1,200 in gross revenue. Yes, more contracts rolled in and income progressed. Eventually. But things got really skinny for a year or two. To boot, I was still paying off college debt, had only a few thousand dollars of savings on hand, and my 401(k) totaled about $5,000.

You can make it without substantial capital reserves. I did. I was also 25 years old, single, and living extremely inexpensively (like a $1,000 per month existence). I didn't have children, either.

The exuberance and joy you have each day for the new endeavor will be tempered with setbacks and missteps. Don't compound the misery by starting off without a firm understanding of financials.

Know Money: Part 2

Before we go any further, understand: Money is not emotional. People are emotional. Money is not, as you've been told, "the root of all evil." Money is merely a medium of exchange that helps us establish value.

While people fester and fantasize about money, it's just an inanimate object created by humans. We use it to determine what something is worth.

As you've read in Part One, we can very simply explain principles of finance. If, coming in to this chapter you were intimidated about money, there is no reason to be so anymore.

Up to now, we covered the basics. Now you're going to hear basics along with a few of my opinions on how to use, handle, and prosper through good money habits. Let's start with borrowing.

Borrowing Money

To begin or expand your empire sometimes requires more money than you have on hand. There are lots of ways to get funding. Before you borrow funds, consider this:

- Debt makes you beholden to someone else or some entity.
- Debt cuts into your creative side. Rather than thinking about the business you're building, you're thinking about how much you owe.
- Debt used indiscriminately distorts reality. Recall the housing bubble when individuals borrowed so much money for homes they couldn't afford, it became more like a Monopoly game than real life? The same goes for government borrowing—can you even comprehend a national debt of $21 trillion?

- Debt can be very useful. Borrowing money to purchase real estate, to buy equipment that will make you money, or for capital improvements that take your business to the next level, makes sense.

> In general, borrow money only for things that make you money or to acquire assets that go up in value.

Now let's talk about the right way to borrow money if necessary.

Establish a Relationship with a Lender

Find a lender you can work with. Yes, relationships matter but don't get rooked—a dollar bill is the truest commodity on earth. Don't pay exorbitant interest to borrow those dollars just because you like your lender.

I personally like dealing with smaller banks. I hate big banks. Our tax dollars bailed out the country's biggest banks a few years ago. I wish all the banks deemed "too big to fail," had. Anyone else see the irony in banks going broke? The same entities that make small-biz people jump through hoops to prove we're worthy of credit can't pay their own bills?

It may take you awhile to find a positive lender relationship. In my early days of self-employment, I had to do all but get a note from my mother and offer to mop the floor of the lobby.

Assuming you do establish a relationship with a lender, promise yourself you will use borrowed money only to grow your empire. Never for shopping trips, vacations, or items that don't produce a return.

Also set up a line of credit for as much as you can get approved for. Hopefully, you will only use this to pounce on opportunities, but you may need funds some month when cash flow is negative.

Credit Cards

Credit cards should be used only as a convenience, never as a source of financing. Pay your cards off every month. This isn't even negotiable.

When you get in the habit of revolving debt on your cards, you stay a revolver on cards. Next thing you know, you're paying 18% interest for a handbag you should never have bought in the first place.

Use credit cards to make payments, not as a loan source.

Venture Capital and Angel Investors

Have you seen the TV show *Shark Tank*? If you don't know what a venture capitalist does or what an angel investor is, watch that show. Granted, it's fluffed up and dramatic for TV, but you'll get the picture.

You, the aspiring entrepreneur, take your idea to someone with money and pitch your idea. The investor bankrolls your venture for a piece of the action. Usually, a significant piece of the action. There's a reason these folks are nicknamed Vulture Capitalists!

If you need money to get your venture off the ground, this might be the only option for you. Be careful. You're attempting to build your own empire. How will you do that when someone else owns 30% to 50% of you?

The Wrap On Borrowing

Remember, when you borrow money, you are obligated to some other person or entity. You work for them! It's completely acceptable to need funding to make your business roll. Just never lose sight of the fact that you went into business for yourself for a reason. It likely wasn't to become an indentured servant. Debt hands over the controls to another party.

Your Business Is Rolling. Now What?

Congratulations. Your business is in the black. Sales are good. Next month looks better than last month. You're on top of the world. Now what do you?

Maximize Revenue

Now that you're prospering, it's critically important that you not take your foot off the gas.

Remember how difficult it was to get here? Recall the struggle and sacrifice you endured to build your business. Don't ever forget the slow times and sacrifice—that'll keep you motivated.

Look around you at the business owners you know who are coasting. They get comfortable, complacent, or downright unmotivated. Their phone is ringing, the email inbox is full of activity, but they're sitting at the coffee shop yakking about nonsense.

As a factory worker, I viewed overtime—when I earned 1.5 or 2 times my normal hourly rate—as the payoff for the hard work during the first 40 hours.

Now look at your business. You did the hard work to get to this point. Now you're working for time and a half or double-time pay. Keep the floodgates of income wide open.

Control Expenses

Controlling outflows in the initial stages of your transformation is easy. You have very little revenue and you're focused on every nickel that goes out the door. When things start cooking it's easy to get sloppy. Don't!

It's reasonable to spend more on your business as you make more. However, the ratio of costs to income should be ratcheting down significantly.

Never Buy Anything without Weighing the ROI

Want to blow a couple hundred bucks on shoes this weekend, fine. You've earned it. But many prospering business owners wreck what they've built by undisciplined spending. You're a business. No shopping trip to the outlet mall with company money!

Businesses must attain a return for the outlay of cash.

Reinvest

You got this far with your product or service, now how can you make it better? Would it be wise to commit some earnings to tweaking the product? Improving your service? Are there capital equipment items that will make you more productive?

How about investing in training and development of your people? This isn't the old days. Change is happening at light speed. There's probably something you can improve upon to make you more salable and more relevant.

Life is about constant learning. If you want to do business better, invest in becoming better.

Don't Buy Anything for the "Tax Write-Off"

You're sitting there on December fifteenth with money in hand, saying, "I should spend this money or I'll be taxed on it."

True. Sometimes and in some ways. A tax write-off should never be the reason for your acquisition of anything. Ask:

Would you buy the item were it not for the tax benefit? Is the tax benefit really that advantageous or are you justifying blowing money?

Continue to Invest in Marketing and Promotion

As revenue grows, it's tempting to say, "Business is good. Why advertise?" Because the world needs to know, with constant reminders, that you exist. That's why.

I know we already covered this in the chapter on promotion but it's worth repeating. Always dedicate a certain amount of your revenue to your brand-building effort. Recall that Coke spends 11% of its revenue on marketing. And Coke is better known than you.

Don't Let Go of the Checkbook

The more successful you become, the more tempting it is to relinquish control of the daily dollars. Don't!

Stories abound of formerly affluent individuals who let go of the checkbook and wound up broke. Professional athletes make for good media in this category but don't kid yourself; there are plenty of small-business people who've been embezzled right out of business.

You're rolling; things are good. At this point, you have plenty of things more important to tend to than filing receipts and cutting checks. Fine. Hire a bookkeeper, but keep your finger on the cash.

Good fences make good neighbors. Financially attentive bosses make honest bookkeepers.

Be Greedy, Not Careless

During boom times, it's easy to spill money out of the buckets you worked so hard to fill. Now's a good time to take the long view and set up systems to prevent you from ending up broke.

First, set a substantial amount of money aside for the potential slow period. Enough to sustain you and your business for three to six months. Touch this money only if absolutely necessary.

Second item, now that you're flying: pay down debt. Remember how we said debt was an obligation. Paying off debt removes the shackles.

Third, when business is booming, raise prices. You'll lose a few customers but they're probably the customers you'd like to lose. In fact, if your price bump doesn't cost you a few of your most difficult, low-margin customers, you might consider firing them.

Good times in business are good times to modify your client base.

Businesspeople fear raising their prices to their own, low profit margin, detriment. Things are booming. Raise your rates.

Wealth Is a Habit

Most money problems are discipline problems, not complex financial matters. You don't need an MBA in finance from an Ivy League school to know you should spend less than you earn.

Wealth is a habit. Money is learnable. If you want to be wealthy, you can be. It just requires discipline.

How to Get Smart About Money

I didn't come from a financially well off background. My parents were blue-collar people and small farmers. They paid their bills, were responsible and hard working, but far from what you'd call sophisticated financiers. I took their examples and built on them through learning. Here are some good sources of education and inspiration regarding money.

The Millionaire Next Door, by Thomas Stanley and William Danko. The authors were professors hired to research the rich. They found a disconnect between the perception of wealth and the reality of wealth. Don't get caught up in the graphs and tables (they're professors).

The Millionaire Mind, by Thomas Stanley. This one is more entertaining than the first. Stories of wealthy, self-made people. I found it inspiring.

The Morgan Stanley Dean Witter Guide to Personal Investing. This is the first book I ever read about investing. Why I liked it? It's simple. So is basic money management and investing. You're not striving to be a Wall Street investment banker dealing in derivatives. And you don't have to be.

Rich Dad, Poor Dad, by Robert Kiyosaki. Don't bother with any of his series after this first (good) book. After his first book's success, he cranked out crap. Read this one and stop. It's worth it.

Actions

19 It's All About *You*

I began this book by stating that I know you. It's true, I do.
I identify with you. I've been you. The aspiring corporate
employee. The hustling, new entrepreneur. The small biz owner
managing operations while not losing the creative edge.

We agreed up front that you were committed to getting
better, to do better. We covered the four unwavering traits
of success. While traits are mostly intrinsic, we discovered
methods to meld success traits into your own personality.

Then we identified the habits of success. Habits, as opposed
to routines, are intentional actions. Good habits as a part of your
daily existence yield prosperity over time.

Now it's time to talk more personally. Now it's up to you. No
traits and no habits will help you do business better if you're
not dialed in.

This final section is all about *you*.

We start by getting you past what's holding you back. Each of
us has something preventing us from being as powerful as we
could be. It's nothing to be ashamed of. Even Superman is ren-
dered useless by Kryptonite. It's time to discover, then dispose
of, your Kryptonite.

Then we determine your business personality. When you're clear about what direction your mind naturally travels, you can profit from it. Alternatively, your productivity will improve as you better understand other people's business personality.

This leads into your talent stack. We'll discover what you're amazing at doing, how to blend that with what you've already done, then capitalize on your synergies.

Humans have big brains. That puts us atop the animal kingdom but it brings big headaches, too. We're emotional. We make bad decisions due to emotion. That's why there's a chapter devoted to understanding your emotions.

When emotion runs your business, emotion ruins your business!

Lastly, we send you out the door with a firm understanding of support. There is supportive behavior and there is enabling behavior. Your success depends on your ability to discern the difference.

Let's start by getting past what's holding you back.

20 Get Past What's Holding You Back

Life gives you baggage. You, me, and every other human on Earth carries baggage. The important thing is to check your bags just like you do at the airport; then hop on the plane for your destination. Unlike flying, you'll be fine if the baggage of your past gets lost!

> Too many people use their past to justify their present and dictate their future.

What Is Holding You Back?

Most people's biggest stumbling block lies in their past. Things that happened decades ago still haunt the individual today.

Are you allowing items from your past to justify your present? Worse yet, dictate your future?

Specifically, name a few things from your past you've struggled to get over. Don't be ashamed. This is cathartic. Acknowledging your personal baggage will make you stronger.

> What items from your past do you allow to hold you back?
>
> _____
>
> _____
>
> _____

I'll help you out here and give you some things that have held me back professionally and personally.

1. I have a chip on my shoulder and a hot temper. This comes from upbringing, birth order, and being a rebellious farm boy of modest means.
2. I'm not a "forgive and forget" kind of person. When I've been wronged, it sticks with me and occupies space in my head.
3. My mother was a negative person who attempted to instill negativity in others. My dark side occasionally wants to have its way.

I know this is an uncomfortable exercise. Growth is uncomfortable. By the end of this chapter, you will be better able to identify what items in your past you're letting sabotage your success.

We'll move on now with things people allow to hold them back.

Back in High School, I Was . . .

Years ago, I attended a three-day seminar in Seattle with two dozen people from all over the country. At dinner, it struck me how some people never get beyond what's holding them back.

A 50-year-old man had been asked about his business and his background. He began his response with, "In high school, I was..." and that's when it turned sad.

Not sad like, "While I was in high school my parents were both killed in an accident so I dropped out of school and took over the family business." That would be sad but also something you'd be proud of a person for overcoming.

His was the story we hear all too often. The story of a person who graduated from high school and 30 years later is still stuck there.

Nerd, jock, zit face, slut, science geek, class clown, shop major, teacher's pet ... we've all been there. Get over it! Stop describing your current self in high school terms. It stunts your growth and impedes your development.

I Lack Education

Speaking of high school. People love to pretend they're not where they should be in life because they have inadequate educational credentials.

For some folks, this is legitimate. For most, it's an excuse.

- You can always get more education. In the era of online courses, you can get an education. Additionally, training options are everywhere.
- If you're not a great student or if you lack the financials, you can still educate yourself. Public libraries have tutors, community colleges have programs to help the disadvantaged, and there's always the option of self-learning with books and online.

People blame their situation on a lack of education because it's easy. What's not so easy is cultivating a habit of lifelong learning.

To clarify, I'm not an education snob. I heard a speaker once refer to himself as having an "Ivy League pedigree." How pretentious. I wanted to smack the arrogant bastard. I'm a "B" student, public school pedigree!

One lesson school didn't teach: Perfect attendance is more important than honor roll. A "C" student who shows up and works can achieve more than a lazy, irresponsible honor student.

Another thought on the topic of education or lack thereof: I know hundreds of people who are self-made success stories who did poorly in school. Or didn't attend college. Or even dropped out of high school. Blame your current situation on a lack of proper schooling if you want. Just know this, many multimillionaires work smarter than their educational credentials would merit.

You Needn't Be Head of the Class

One of the wealthiest individuals I personally know is a guy from Michigan named Dave. He's been a client multiple times. I've stayed in two or three of his homes. Our relationship began in my political comedy days. A company he owns hired me to entertain their sales conference and then hired me again. Then he booked me for a private party at one of his country clubs. Then there were philanthropic fundraisers, and so on.

Dave hired me to be the entertainment for his class reunion, too. He hosted the reunion at a golf course and banquet facility he owns. In prepping for the show, I asked how many kids were in his high school class. "There were 64 kids in our class," he replied. "I graduated 62nd."

This man is worth multiples of millions of dollars. He runs several companies, sits on boards of publicly traded corporations, and has various other business interests. Yet, he was almost dead last in his high school class.

My Parents Didn't...

Some people just can't get past their upbringing. But you have to.

If you were abused, I sincerely apologize. I credit you for working to get beyond that to be a better human.

I'm not talking about parental criminality. I'm talking about parental bad habits. Many people use their parent's habits as an excuse for their own lack of achievement.

"My parents didn't teach me about money." "My parents were bad role models." "My parents didn't work hard."

News flash: *Leave It to Beaver* was a TV show. Sorry your upbringing wasn't ideal. Neither was anyone else's. You're an adult now. Stop blaming your parents and vow to make better decisions than they did.

My Friends and Family Drag Me Down

Humans are social animals. We form family units and friendships. When we better ourselves we make those around us look bad.

Our peers don't want to look like underachievers. They don't want to do the hard work of self-betterment, either.

So, what do they do? They snipe. They discourage your progress. They caution you against risk. Advise you to stop working so hard. Discount your ideas. Worst of all, folks you've known your whole life sabotage your advancement.

Why? Because it's easier to keep you at their level than for them to raise their own game.

Name the friends and family members who drag you
down:

_____

_____

_____

How to Get Past What's Holding You Back

All of us have our human limitations. Your goal is to go beyond
those barriers—oftentimes self-imposed barriers—to attain
what you want. On your terms. Here's how you get past what's
holding you back.

Realize That Most People Don't Care

The limitations and self-doubt you carry around with you are
yours. They're in your head. Most people don't care, don't
remember, or don't know anything about your past. Stop
obsessing over it. Show the world what you are today. Yesterday
doesn't matter.

Every time your past is weighing you down, think about this:
There are 7.5 billion humans on Earth. Whatever you're hung
up on isn't even on the minds of all those billions of people.

Cut Out the "Diminishers" (Yes, I Made That Word Up!)

People who bring up negative aspects of your past do so to
diminish you. It makes them feel superior to rub in your face
that you were poor, or a bad student, or went through a difficult
time professionally.

Some "diminishers" pass their behavior off as humor as they ridicule you. It's not funny; it's posturing. An attempt to heighten themselves by diminishing you. Cut "diminishers" out of your life immediately.

Because I'm the independent, self-made, outspoken sort, I deal with more than my fair share of diminishers. Sometimes they're motivated by envy. Others find joy in taking shots at the high-profile guy.

I cut contact with those who seek to diminish me. You should do the same. Generally, diminishers reference items from your history in their effort to defame and disgrace. If you're like me, you don't need to be reminded that at age 21 you were a directionless, depressed, penniless underachiever.

> Life takes energy. Do you want to spend that energy defending your history or creating your future?

Let Your Background Motivate You

We don't live in a caste system. We don't do royalty. There are no serfs, peasants, or kings.

I'll stop short of saying you can be whatever you want to be. Frankly, I bristle when rah-rah motivational types say such things. If you're 40 years old, 5'7" and can't jump, you can't be a professional basketball player. But you can be wildly successful and exceedingly happy.

Don't let others lock you in a stratum of social and economic underachievement. More importantly, don't allow your own insecurities to do it either.

America has a rich heritage of self-made people who came from nothing. Enjoy country music? Think of Dolly Parton, the girl raised in a family of 12 in a Tennessee shack. Coffee more your taste? How about Howard Schultz of Starbucks, who was raised in the projects of Brooklyn.

Admittedly, there is economic evidence that America is not as upwardly mobile as it has been in the past. You can't fix the wealth distribution curve. But you can do your part to climb higher than where you started from.

Move

Nothing brings perspective to a problem like a little distance. Maybe what's holding you back is your environment. Move!

A new location brings new connections, new stimuli, and most importantly, new opportunities. People complain about their situation, their job, and their location routinely. Those things are changeable.

One note, though: A change in zip codes won't fix your self-imposed immobility. Get your head straight and then head for greener pastures. Because you can run from your past, but you can't hide from yourself!

> You can run from your past but you can't hide from yourself!

Terminate Some Professional Relationships

To make progress, you must be willing to grow out of relationships. Both business and personal. Let's talk business first.

Your existing client base has you pigeonholed. To them, you are what you've always been. It requires a tremendous effort for clientele to see you in a different light. Most never will.

That's why most people don't change much. Because they don't have the fortitude to cultivate new clients for their new offering. Safer and easier to just stay pigeonholed and stick with what you've always done.

The clients and agencies I worked with in my political comedy days couldn't wrap their head around me being a business speaker and writer.

When I (painfully) run into colleagues from my days as a sales rep, they go right back to 1993 and talk about the light fixture business. How dark! Yes, the pun was intentional.

You don't want to be what you've always been. That's why you're reading this book. You want to bump it up a level or two (or 10!). To do that, you need to fire your old customers. Alter your business mix. Develop new clients who see you as what you are, not what you were.

Even Good Clients Can Hold You Back

A few pages back, I told you about my former client, Dave. The guy is a huge fan and he's fantastically wealthy. One of my best repeat clients. He's no longer a client and he likely will never be again. Not because we had a falling out. We didn't. I just moved on and he didn't move with me.

To Dave, I'm a political comedian who delivers a show in the persona of Bill Clinton. I don't do that anymore. Dave owns several companies. He could hire me to speak to his sales force on doing business better. But he probably won't. Because to him, I'll always be Bill Clinton. There's no demand for that anymore. More importantly, *I don't want to do that anymore*!

(continued)

(*continued*)

In show biz, it's called being typecast. A few paragraphs back, I called it being pigeonholed. Whatever you call it, every business suffers from it.

We all have customers who love us. As long as we don't change. Then they go from being awesome clients to anchors holding us back. They don't want anything special. They just want you to do what you always used to do. Back in the "good old days." For the same money, of course, that you always did it for, even though that's half what you're charging nowadays.

Fire them. Move on. Even good clients can hold you back.

Service Providers Too

You'll have to change service providers too. Your old accountant who did your taxes over beers at Applebee's can't scale up. You have 200 employees and you're grossing millions.

The equipment dealer you bought your first mower from as a 16-year-old cutting the neighbor's yard? You're a full-blown landscape company now with a dozen crews. Time for a vendor change.

Your quest is prosperity and happiness. To achieve that, you must get past what's holding you back. Your banker, insurance lady, CPA, investment advisor, business consultant...while these relationships may be comfortable, that doesn't mean they aren't holding you back.

What professional relationships are holding you back?

Do customers/clients have you pigeonholed? What do they see you as?

Is your business stunted because you keep giving old customers what they want rather than moving forward?

What current service providers lack scale or sophistication to help you get where you're going?

Sever Harmful Personal Relationships

Severing personal relationships is even more critical than cutting professional relationships.

Do you really have much in common with that old roommate from college? The girl your locker was next to in eighth grade whose life is a disaster today? No, you don't.

Worse yet, some people from your past are toxic. They drag drama to your doorstep, then you open the door to let it in. Why? Because you've always done it. You've always been there to let these draining people drag you down to their level. End it!

Misery loves company. It's easier to find someone to commiserate with than it is to get off one's ass and change one's situation. Stop being the company that misery loves to keep.

I heard a nationally recognized poverty expert speak at a conference where I too was speaking. Her research finds that some in the impoverished class really don't want their offspring to succeed. Because, their reasoning goes, when little Johnny does well through education, hard work, and good habits, he leaves the nest.

Impoverished parents don't want to lose a relationship with their children. So some of these parents sabotage the success of their offspring. How tragically sad.

Now ask yourself a question: Do you have people trying to keep you unaccomplished so they won't lose you? Trust me, you do. We all do.

Don't allow these people to derail you. Sever damaging relationships. It's time to move beyond those who stunt your growth.

Recall a few pages back when I asked you to name your peers who drag you down? Did you actually put names on the page? It's time to cut those people off. Sure, it's uncomfortable. Growth is uncomfortable. You absolutely must drop relationships that are holding you back.

What personal relationships are you going to sever for your self-betterment?

_____

_____

Two Kinds of People

There are two kinds of people: those who cheer on your success and those who resent your achievement.

Seek out those who cheer you on. Terminate relationships with those who diminish you for your accomplishments. Become a person who celebrates achievement in your own life as well as others.

Have you ever heard your income will average that of your five closest colleagues? Turns out, birds of a feather truly do flock together. Spend time with those who motivate you, not those who hold you back.

People Who Focus on What's Behind Them Fall Down!

When I hear people say, "If I had it to do over again, I wouldn't change a thing," I think, are you stupid? I'd change lots of things! But we can't.

We can't alter items in our past that we carry around as baggage. All we can do is check our baggage.

> Successful people shed habits, hang-ups, and relationships that are holding them back. It's time for you to move forward.

21 Your Business Personality

Successful people make a habit of understanding and working within their business personality.

Business personality, you say? Yes. It's like your "personality" personality except it presents itself in how you work. Similar to your personal personality, changing your business personality is difficult. It's who you are.

You need to understand your business personality so you can capitalize on it. In some cases, work around it, if necessary.

The Five P's

In Marketing 101 they teach the Four P's of the marketing mix: Product, Price, Place, and Promotion.

Playing off of that, I developed what I call the Five P's of Business Personality: *Product, Process, People, Promotion,* and *Profitability.*

You probably identify with aspects of all of these traits. Good. You should. Because each of them is important to running your own endeavor. Eventually you'll discover—and maybe you already have—you're strong at a couple of the P's and struggle with the others.

That's okay. Knowing your business personality is half the battle. Exploiting it for success is the other half. Let's cover the five elements of business personality.

Product

A lot of people think a really good product is all that matters. They're wrong. The DeLorean was a good car. It was stainless steel in the era of rust bucket automobiles. Remember Ziebart rust protection?

The DeLorean was peppy, efficient, and cool to look at. The car had a role in one of the best films of the 1980s, *Back to the Future*. But John DeLorean's company never turned a profit.

Conversely, Chick fil-A is the most profitable per-outlet fast food chain. Is it because their chicken sandwich is a really good product? Maybe. I don't know. I can get only so excited about a chicken sandwich.

I'm inclined to say the sandwiches are fine. But Chick fil-A's profitability is more due to a keen grasp of process, promotion, and people.

See how this works? How they all tie together?

Let's talk about product: it's square one. Your business doesn't exist without a service or good to sell. It can be tangible or intangible. A staple gun is tangible. Your wisdom as a ski coach is intangible.

For sure, your product must meet certain criteria. The staple gun must shoot staples to accomplish the objective of binding things. Your ski tutoring must help clients slide down a snowy hill better than they did before meeting you.

The problem arises when you think product is *all* that matters. Yes, work to make your offering better. But focusing 100 percent of your effort on product leaves too many other items to fall through the cracks.

Perfection Isn't One of the Five P's! You needn't be obsessive about product perfection to attain success.

We discussed this up front when I told you to get better, not perfect. It's okay to pursue perfection. But don't wait until your product is perfect before selling it or you'll be out of business before you start.

Remember: Most products are acceptable, not perfect. Want proof?

Microsoft Windows was never perfect. Yet Bill Gates is one of the richest humans on Earth. Millions of people live in imperfectly constructed tract-style homes. I've yet to drive a perfect car. Pepsi is inferior to Coke (if you disagree with me on this point, we will simply never get along!). Okay, let's not start another cola war. The point is, perfection is a difficult, and often unprofitable, pursuit.

Next up . . . process.

Process

How projects get done matters. Although not necessarily to me. Procedures remind me of rulebooks. Procedures remind me of reading directions. Rules and directions are two things I generally avoid! Therefore, I'm not a process person. Maybe you are.

Process-minded people tend to be "by the book" types. Methods matter to these people.

I had an agent who was a process personality type. He called himself "detail oriented." I called him an annoying pain in the ass. I used to make the mistake of bouncing creative concepts off him. After a few years, it became apparent that ideas were as foreign as Swahili to this guy.

Processors crush creativity unknowingly. While the visionary's mind is on a creative tear, jotting images on the whiteboard, the processor is thinking about which government forms need to be filled out.

I once worked in a ceiling tile factory. I appreciate the efficiency of process. I just don't want to be that person. Whereas shaving three seconds off the manufacture of each ceiling tile is the sort of thing process personalities dream of.

Process people struggle when they have to go "off script" as we say in showbiz. Protocols are great when the world throws you textbook challenges. But what do you do when faced with a problem that didn't make the owner's manual?

This is why I encourage business people to make a habit of making themselves uncomfortable.

> Process becomes routine.
> Routine becomes mindless!

People

Lots of folks say, "I'm a people person."

I'm convinced they say this out of fear they'll be labeled anti-social. Spend time interacting with people. Buy from them. Be "served" by them. Soon, you too will question the validity of "people person" claims.

I'm not a people person. This surprises most folks who assume a comedy background requires people ability. In truth, most professionally funny individuals I know are secretly introverted, verging on misanthropic.

Here's the reality: we all work for other people. Which means, we have no choice but to be people people. I'll remind you again of this fundamental business fact: Every dollar in existence that you don't currently possess is held by someone else.

Business success requires a certain amount of People business personality. Admittedly, sometimes you have to force your people person-ness.

Other times, you have to be firm. Extreme "people persons" get taken advantage of by employees, clients, service providers, and everyone else. Because humans generally don't do what's right; they do what they can get away with. It's sad but true, if you're too nice, you will get railroaded.

Conversely, we all know individuals who should be kept as far from humans as humanly possible! Yet, some companies stick their sourpusses on the front line. What does that do? Tanks the business, that's what.

A Bad Act

Two aspiring business owners renovated an old movie theater and began theatrical dinner productions. This was neat to see in a factory and farm town. My wife and I approached the owners immediately to pledge our financial support. Which we did for several years. Until one night when the worst people person at the theater caused me to drop the curtain.

The owner's mom had a unique personality. By "unique," I mean "bitchy." For some reason they put her in a role interfacing with customers. Lori and I were seated at a table with complete strangers. When we inquired about a change of table, we were berated.

(continued)

(*continued*)

We never went back. Not even for the productions we already bought tickets to. We stopped supporting the theater from that point forward. The dinner theater closed. I'm sure the owners cite market limitations as the reason.

Most of us sell things that aren't necessities. Even if we *are* selling necessities, there are plenty of other providers. Don't make the mistake of thinking the customer can't live without you.

Promotion

If you don't have Promotion in your DNA, hire someone who does. It's that important.

Contrary to popular misconception, no good idea ever sold itself. In fact, brilliant ideas terrify uncreative, risk-averse sorts. Therefore, brilliant ideas require triple the promotion.

Recall Apple's Steve Jobs? He had an amazing mind. He was also an amazing promoter. Remember how artfully he worked the media to cover his new product launches? That's a professional promoter.

Steve Jobs gets accolades and respect. Ringmaster P.T. Barnum, on the other hand, is jeered as a circus act. He, too, was a professional promoter.

Promoters come in a lot of packages. They're not known for *being* promoters, they're known because they *are* promoters.

Donald Trump promoted himself to the presidency. Kim Kardashian made a career out of self-promotion.

Car Salesmen

Lee Iacocca is credited with creating the Mustang (he didn't) and saving Chrysler (the first time). He didn't do that, either. Both times Chrysler was saved by your tax dollars. But Lee had a best-selling business book long before the Jack Welches of the world made it popular for biz execs to be authors. Why do people believe Mr. Iacocca was responsible for the Mustang and bailing out Chrysler? Because he told people he was.

Enter Elon Musk. Last I looked, Tesla's stock price had the company valued at $19 billion more than Ford. Did you hear that? Ford. Henry's company (also a pretty damn good promoter) sells more F-150s in a month than Tesla's total car production since its inception. So why is Tesla so valuable? Because Mr. Musk goes on TV and the Internet. He paints a glowing vision of a future where humans bop around outer space in one of his shiny cars. That's promotion.

Now do you understand the value of promotion? Good. Now let's talk about the damage of negative promotion.

Every person you employ is on the promotion team. How they talk about you and your company away from work is promotion or sabotage. The same with how they interact with customers. Promotion or sabotage. Remember the theater owner's mom? Bad people personality, bad promotion personality.

Profitability

We talked up front about the benefits of being money minded. When it comes to your business personality, what's your Profitability rating? I'll help you figure this out by asking a few questions.

- What are your fixed business expenses?
- Variable business expenses?
- What did you gross last year? How does that compare with the prior year?
- Where do you have the greatest likelihood of increasing revenue?
- Where are you spending more money than the current return justifies?
- What is your personal net worth?

If you're saying, "Damian, this is rudimentary financial stuff," congratulations. You rank high on the Profit personality type. If those questions sent you into a panic, you need to foster your profit personality.

You might be saying, "Damian, I'm gonna make so much money it won't matter!"

Really? Like Wayne Newton, for instance? He's Mr. Las Vegas—more aptly named Mr. Financial Fiasco. Some estimates put Wayne's annual earnings at $25 million. Yet he's been in and out of personal bankruptcy and sued by creditors, despite being a showbiz icon with sold-out shows. Wayne even had an ongoing court battle over the value of a horse!

Why You Need Profit in Your Business Personality Profile
Business ventures embarked on by those without a Profit personality often falter.

Product types focus like a laser on their amazing widget, never realizing it costs more to make than it can be sold for.

Processors dial in on how things get done. But even if the operation is seamless, that doesn't guarantee you'll be financially in the black.

People personality types take financial misfortune personally. "How could the world do this to me? I'm a good person."

Promoters are sometimes so convincing, they convince themselves they needn't worry about profitability. Wayne Newton's picture was emblazoned on the casino marquee and the roof of every cab in Vegas. But he was broke.

> Your business doesn't serve you, nor can it serve others, if it's not profitable!

Biz Personality Test

If you've ever taken a personality test, you know nobody is 100% of anything. Introvert, extrovert, aesthetic, driver, amiable, leader, follower . . . Most of us gravitate hard in one or two personality directions with hints of other traits.

So it is with your business personality. You're complex. Yet your mind tilts in a pronounced manner in one or two directions. Which ones?

Grading Your Business Personality

Using a system of 1–100, rate your business personality. Don't worry, your grade won't be graded. The goal of the exercise is to clearly and honestly examine yourself. When you know your Biz Personality, you can manage for results.

So you won't feel like you're taking the test alone, I'll give you my grades to the right of yours.

Product_____Damian = 75
Process_____Damian = 10
People_____Damian = 50
Promotion____Damian = 80
Profit_____Damian = 90

22 Exploiting Your Talent Stack

J ust like your business personality tilts in different directions, you have varying degrees of skill elsewhere. Your skill may be natural or it may be through diligent effort. Doesn't matter how you got your tools; it matters how you employ them.

We'll refer to your entire combination of skills and attributes as your talent stack. I can't take credit for that term. The "talent stack" concept was created by the same guy who created *Dilbert,* the comic strip character.

In his book, *Win Bigly,* Scott Adams of *Dilbert* fame alludes to "talent stack." He coined the term in an earlier book, *How to Fail at Almost Everything and Still Win Big.*

The Talent Stack Concept by Scott Adams

There are two ways to make yourself valuable:

1. Be the best in the world at one thing, which is very difficult to do.
2. Develop a variety of skills that work well together, thereby creating synergy.

Mr. Adams uses himself as an example. He says:

I'm a famous syndicated cartoonist who doesn't have much artistic talent, and I've never taken a college-level writing class. But few people are good at both drawing and writing. When you add in my ordinary business skills, my strong work ethic, my risk tolerance, and my reasonably good sense of humor, I'm fairly unique. And in this case that uniqueness has commercial value.

From Scott Adams to a different Scott, my good friend since high school. Scott and I were roommates during our early professional days. He was a law student and budding attorney. I was a comedic Bill Clinton impersonator. My act included pretend Secret Service men. I enlisted Scott, and other friends, for the role.

After working his 100th show, Scott said to me, "Damian, I've seen your act more than anyone. I also watch you run your business. On stage you're a "B," but you're an "A" at your desk."

I wasn't insulted. His observation motivated me to keep improving the act. That's called focusing on the product.

I also wasn't insulted because Scott was right. I was better at my desk than I was on stage. That's the promotion and profit part of my business personality profile.

Since then, I've expanded on Scott's observation. I tell folks to succeed in showbiz, understand this: There are four letters in "show," eight letters in "business." Apply effort proportionally.

Synergy of the Stack

The concept of the Talent Stack is that you don't need to be amazing at any one thing. You simply need to be above average at many things that feed one another.

Mr. Adams includes things you wouldn't normally call "talent." By his description, physical features, past jobs, experiences, education, social skills, humor, and other attributes count as talent.

After reading about the talent stack, I did a self-analysis. Then I reflected on my friend Scott's feedback from so many years ago.

Undeniably, I'm an A+ at nothing, but a solid B at multiple things. Fusing them all together has been the key to any success I've attained.

What's Your Talent Stack?

What variety of skills and attributes that work well together can you capitalize on?

I know you're shy, so I'll go first. Here's my talent stack:

- Work Ethic
- Salesmanship
- Energy Level
- Memory
- Observation
- Humor
- Public Speaking

List your talent stack

_____

_____

_____

_____

Background and Upbringing

Struggling to define your talent stack? I'll help you find your skills that work well together with a simple exercise. But first, read this about background and upbringing. In analyzing your own background and upbringing, you'll discover some strengths you forgot about.

While these aren't skills, they are big contributors to my talent stack. Probably for you, too.

Upbringing You can choose to use your upbringing as an excuse or inspiration. Just understand, there's no such thing as a perfect background and all families are dysfunctional. Why? Because humans are imperfect and dysfunctional.

We can't change the past but we can mine your upbringing for nuggets of gold to apply to your talent stack. I'll go first, then it's your turn.

I was raised the youngest of nine children in a household of hotheads. Conflict doesn't faze me. I learned to navigate diverse personalities with divergent objectives. As the littlest, I absorbed how members of a large group jockey to get their way.

Early on, I grasped the need to understand one's position. When you're overpowered, use intellect. Outsmarted? Bring force. Outmoneyed? Bring personality. In everything you do, bring creativity and energy.

My upbringing taught me that those who are older and bigger than you don't perceive you as a threat until it's too late. This lesson applies to every start-up company dominated by old, stodgy monoliths. (Do you think any boardroom in America perceived Google as a threat early on?)

I credit my sense of timing to being youngest. Getting attention and laughs requires impeccable timing at a noisy dinner table.

The gold from my upbringing: understanding group dynamics, conflict and resolution, capitalizing on position, and comedic timing.

What nuggets can you mine from your upbringing to contribute to your talent stack?

_____

_____

_____

_____

_____

Background Background, for the purpose of this exercise, refers to the people you've interacted with, the jobs you've had, and socioeconomic factors that sculpted you. We're looking for takeaways to build upon your talent stack. My background is rich with lessons. Yours probably is too.

Farm As a child I handled large animals and ran powerful farm machinery. I worked alongside grown-ups from the time I was 8. Because of this, not much intimidates me.

Rail In addition to the farm, my dad worked second shift as a railroad crew dispatcher. The men he called to crew the trains genuinely liked my dad. Sometimes when their number was called (way before cellphones!), they were drunk in a bar. Or shacked up at their girlfriend's place. Or otherwise missing in action. My dad found them, sobered them up, or covered for them.

Every Christmas there were a dozen gift boxes of booze under our tree from grateful railroaders. This was a year's supply for my dad—he didn't drink like the average railroader!

Twice my dad got injured on the farm. The injuries caused him to miss his job for extended periods. Twice the railroaders came to visit with a stack of cash they'd collected for our family. From this I learned the value of relationships and being respected.

Factory   At 18, I got my factory job. Working the midnight shift in a dusty mill with an assortment of characters—including ex-convicts—was invaluable. The factory taught me manufacturing. I participated in the value-added process. At one end of the plant we started with a pile of rock and clay. At the other end of the plant, we cranked out boxes of pretty ceiling tile.

Mostly, the factory taught me about people. I witnessed the precarious situation of unskilled manufacturing employees. I learned what happens when management is chosen by marriage, rather than merit. I saw the disparity in thinking, from the line to management. The factory taught me to respect every person, regardless of intelligence or rank, if they're willing to show up and work.

Bar   Years ago, I studied improvisational acting at Second City. We were assigned to act out a bar scene. The younger students played the bar patrons as stupid and clumsy. The instructor cut the scene and explained some pure wisdom. "Drunks aren't stupid. They're honest!" he exclaimed.

He was right. I already knew this because I worked in bars long before taking improv classes. Alcohol is truth serum. A person described as a "mean drunk" is mean—it just requires booze for the truth to surface. Working in the bar business showed me humans have a very ugly side. All it takes to reveal Mr. Hyde is truth serum.

Like Upbringing, you can use Background as either an excuse or inspiration. My talent stack is enhanced by the experiences of my background. What about yours?

What lessons from your background could contribute to your talent stack?

_____

_____

_____

_____

Discovering Your Talent Stack

Now it's time for the exercise I promised. We're going to discover your talent stack.

Your Talent Stack Revealed

What Do You Do Now? What Is Your Job or Business?

_____

_____

_____

List Every Way You Earn Money

I'm not asking to be nosy. I'm asking because the Talent Stack concept is about adding value to yourself. How you earn money and how much money you earn reflects value according to the marketplace.

So, list your job, business ownership, investments, royalties, consulting, and so on....

_____

_____

_____

(continued)

(continued)

List Every Job You've Had, and the Lessons You Learned from That Job

Every job you've had is job training for the next one. Especially if you're smart enough to observe and learn on the job.

_____

_____

_____

The entrepreneurial mind doesn't just show up and work for a paycheck. The entrepreneur works for knowledge *and* a paycheck. If you're still traditionally employed contemplating entrepreneurialism, train yourself to be an on-the-job observer.

How did or does your employer add value?

_____

_____

_____

How did or does the employer manage people?

_____

_____

_____

How did or does your employer treat customers?

_____

_____

_____

What lesson (or bad example) did you glean from a co-worker that you've applied to your own career?

_____

_____

_____

What wisdom did you glean about the Five P's? Especially people? (Think of my factory example.)

_____

_____

_____

Education

Write down everything from your GED to PhD. Every subject you mastered; every seminar you paid to attend; every course you took for accreditation.

If you're a lifelong learner, write down a course you took or a book you read that impacted your life or work. My list would include my formal education, of course, but also: soils analysis, improv training, benefit auctioneer school, Professional Sales 431, and a multitude of books.

It might even be helpful to asterisk subjects you were particularly good at or specifically interested in.

Education:

_____

_____

_____

(continued)

(*continued*)

What Are the Constants in Your Life?

What were you raised around that impacted you? For me, it was the farm, a large family, and the blue-collar environment.

Was there a family business? Remember my farm example? What's yours?

Where were you raised that might provide a unique angle compared to others?

I'll give you an example from the world of comedy: Richard Pryor. Granted, he had some bad habits, like drug use. Richard also had some good habits, like work ethic. Richard was raised in Peoria, Illinois, and used his upbringing as stage material. He possessed a genuine Midwest work ethic regarding material development and honing his act.

In a book I read about Mr. Pryor, the author noted that for an entire week he watched Richard on stage. Pryor never did the same act twice. He changed it slightly, massaging the material to perfect it, and constantly rolling out new material.

Recall the chapter on drive? Does comedy legend Richard Pryor fit that?

What gold can you pan from your roots?

_____

_____

_____

What Are Your Interests? Hobbies?

This is easy: analyze your week and clock where you spend your time. Where you spend your time, energy, and money is what you care about. Disagree all you like but there's no hiding from the truth of time, energy, and money.

If you spend five hours per night watching TV (most people do), you're interested in being a couch potato. More positively, if you spend your time tuning piano, remodeling your home, or cultivating your garden, you might just have discovered an element of your talent stack.

What are your interests?

_____

_____

_____

Skills, Strengths, and Expertise

What are you better at than most people? There's no prize for being humble. There's also no prize for over-confidence. Where are you above average?

List your strengths. Anything that's a 'B+' or higher qualifies.

_____

_____

_____

_____

Physical Attributes

It's up to you whether you list anything here. Shallow or not, physical attributes matter. Being big has helped a lot of pro athletes make money. Being small is a bonus for gymnasts and jockeys. A distinctive look

(continued)

(*continued*)

has been leveraged by many a celebrity, from the afore-mentioned Kim Kardashian to Conan O'Brien.

To give you a personal example: I'm taller than average with a raspy voice and I stay fit. Those things have some benefit for a professional speaker.

Do you have any physical qualities that contribute to your talent stack?

_____

_____

_____

Stack 'Em Up!

What attributes did you discover that can benefit your life and career? Either flip back a few pages where I asked you to write down your talent stack or start over here.

What skills do you have that would work well together? (Remember, some items on the list may not be "skills" in the traditional sense.)

_____

_____

_____

Congruence: the quality or state of agreeing or corresponding

Intentional: done with intention or on purpose

Intentional Congruence

A few years ago I attended a business improvement session with the National Speakers Association. A speaker and author named Nido Qubein was one of the presenters. He introduced me to the concept of Intentional Congruence.

Nido's definition is more lengthy than we'll get into here but the gist is this: Where do things in your life, work, values, interests, and connections align?

The idea is to intentionally align one's life and business so that each circle overlaps and feeds the other.

Sound a bit like Mr. Adams's concept of Talent Stack?

Success comes from intentionally applying your attributes in a coordinated and congruent manner.

You'll Use Everything You've Ever Learned

A couple more showbiz examples.

In Steve Martin's book, *Born Standing Up,* he describes his first appearance on *The Tonight Show* with Johnny Carson.

After delivering his set, the show cut to commercial. Steve was approached by Johnny Carson. The show biz legend told Steve Martin, "You'll use everything you've ever learned in this business."

The point Mr. Carson was making: Comedic entertainment is difficult work. I can relate. I've done it. Albeit not as famously as either of these two guys. Johnny Carson was right. To be successful, you use everything you know. I've pulled out data, jokes, and references I thought I'd forgotten—during the heat of the moment.

Previously, we covered Lady Gaga. Do you suppose today, Gaga still pulls lessons from her background? You bet she does.

Those nights of schlepping her keyboard around clubs in New Jersey? The low-paying gigs she did as a teenager when she learned nuances of performing. Do you think working as a go-go dancer taught her anything?

At the time of this writing, Lady Gaga has a net worth of $275 million. Yet she still works with her voice coach. Still learning.

> Why would the notion of using everything you've ever learned apply only to showbiz and not YOUR BIZ?

Your Talent Stack Is Your Toolbox

If you want to be successful, possess a deep toolbox. As I said in the opening paragraph of this chapter, it doesn't matter how you got your tools; it matters how you employ them.

To be successful, you'll use everything you've ever learned!

23 Manage Your Emotions

Humans are emotional beasts. You're not an exception. So please know this: when you allow emotion to run your business, emotion will ruin your business.

Let's Talk About Emotions

Emotional complexity is what separates us from the lesser animals. We learned this in high school biology, didn't we? I was 15. My hormones had me so whacked out and emotional, it's amazing I can even remember such things. Now we're adults. It's time to supplement the lessons from biology class. Especially as it relates to our feelings and our business.

This chapter is devoted to human emotion. How you manage your feelings *will* impact your business and your finances.

The Emotional Impediment

A huge impediment to success and happiness for most people is unchecked emotion.

Don't tell me, "Damian, I'm a very sensitive individual." Great. The more you allow yourself that excuse, the worse off you'll be.

I comprehend the emotion that comes from creating and running one's own empire. I do it. And I run pretty hot. My wife jokes that my business is hard work and creativity, punctuated with a daily tirade.

You're entitled to an occasional meltdown. Just don't allow your business to resemble a teenage love affair. Drama is exhausting. Bad for business, too, because you'll make bad decisions.

Still convinced you're too sensitive for emotional management? Understand this: I know lots of artistic types. The prosperous ones channel their emotion to achieve the desired outcome of their creation. Then they put on their business owner hat and distance themselves from their feelings.

In short, the more consumed you are by your feelings, the harder to achieve balance and prosperity.

Big Girls Do Cry

Believe it or not, big girls and boys do cry. Which is why I'll give you permission to be emotional. I just won't give you permission to run your business emotionally. There's a difference.

This is your business. You invented it, reinvented it, ran it through fat and through lean. It's your baby. I'm right there with you. I've cried, screamed, cussed, and sweated over my endeavors. Still do.

In running your own enterprise you will celebrate the highest highs and endure some of your lowest lows. You're fully vested. This isn't just a part-time job you took for an extra buck. It's yours. In many ways it's who you are, too. Regardless, you can't let your feelings wreck the future and the finances of your business.

Know Your Emotions

You should know who you are and how you work. Back in ninth grade biology class you couldn't control some of your adolescent urges. It was all new. Now you're an adult. You know what makes you go. You also know your weak spots. If you don't, you should.

We're going to find your weak spots in this exercise. To help you out, I'll go first.

My Weak Spots I'm impatient. Also hotheaded. I'm prone to stress, which disrupts my sleep when projects are not completed. I like my life, surroundings, and business to be in order. Disarray is the devil. I'm also ADHD. This requires management for emotional health so I can focus to complete work. Because if I don't, I fester all night over things being in disarray.

There. I just explained me. You need to do the same.

What do you know about yourself and your emotions?

_____

_____

_____

Manage Your Emotions

Feelings are powerful. Ever hear of a "crime of passion"? They don't use that term to describe jaywalking. It refers to murder committed because of love or lust. That's powerful stuff.

We all have this emotional beast within us, capable of turning on us at any moment. What should you do? Manage your emotional state like you're managing warehouse inventory. Meaning unemotionally.

This is where most folks fail. They know their emotions but lack discipline to check and balance them. Ever see a little kid throwing a tantrum at the grocery store? That's you when you allow feelings to get in front of your finances.

To be clear, we are talking about managing your emotional state, not managing mental illness. Mental illness is a serious issue. Thankfully, mental illness is losing the stigma and getting the attention it deserves.

I'm good friends with a couple of psychiatrists. I haven't the credentials to do their job. But I can help you put your emotions in proper perspective so you'll have a thriving business.

How to Tame Your Emotional Beast

First off, realize that most people don't care about you or your feelings. Sure, your friends do, but they're probably not paying customers.

Friends Influence Your Feelings

A note on the issue of friends and feelings: who you choose to spend time with and what you get out of those encounters will either make you or break you. If your time with friends resembles a soap opera, turn off the TV! Drama creates drama.

In the chapter "Get Past What's Holding You Back," we discussed people in your life who are holding you back. If you want to prosper personally and professionally, rid your life of emotional basket cases. They're never going to get better. Their only purpose is to drag you into their drama.

Back to the point about nobody caring about your feelings. They don't. They're your paying clients. They aren't paying for your happiness; they're paying to increase their happiness.

> People care about themselves. Never forget that.

Second, emotional management is life management. For example, here are my techniques:

I exercise almost every day. This helps focus, which increases productivity. I sleep better at night. It keeps me fit. Emotionally *and* physically.

Money is important to me. As it is to you! Therefore, I manage money to alleviate stress. I want financial solvency for the freedom from worry it buys.

Are you getting the point? Your emotional state is oftentimes a result of what you do or don't do with your time and energy. For me, it's physical exertion, money management, focus, and work completion.

> Write down three action steps you will take to manage your emotional beast:
>
> 1. _____
> 2. _____
> 3. _____

Facts Don't Matter

It's a fact, people make almost every decision based on emotion, then back it up with facts. They won't tell you they do this, but they do.

The facts don't even have to be accurate. Because facts don't matter in an emotional decision and most decisions are made by emotion.

Vehicles, political candidates, organic food, clothing, even investments—all emotional choices for most people.

Enterprise Calling Spock

You make decisions every day. Some of them are one-dollar decisions; others might be million-dollar decisions. You can get emotional over choices that cost you a buck. But you never do. It's the big-money decisions where emotion wreaks havoc. Don't let it. Here's how.

When you're faced with a big decision, put all the data on the table.

Now remove emotion from the room. This is easier said than done when there's a lot on the line. Trust me, I've been there! Purchasing farms, revamping my product offering, huge investments on business expansion—all stressful decisions. It's easy for an outsider to tell you not to worry. But you're the one losing sleep, with indigestion, who feels like your hair is falling out.

This is when you've gotta find your Mr. Spock. Yes, I'm referring to the old *Star Trek* episodes because they're awesome. Spock is a Vulcan. He doesn't possess feelings, only logic. Pull yourself back from every decision and ask, "What would the smartest person on the *USS Enterprise* do, minus the emotion?"

In other words, imagine you are a completely unrelated entity viewing this decision through an unemotional lens. Then what would you do?

It's *Your Enterprise*

"But Damian," you shriek, "people's lives will be impacted by my decision!" Yep. So will yours. In fact, your life is already impacted. Because it's *your* business. You've already festered and contemplated the outcomes more than all the people you're worried about put together.

I willingly admit I struggle as an employer. Call it the curse of the self-employed. Human resources is my weakness. I once had an absolute disaster of an employee. She lied about her competencies, didn't take instruction well, and was combative at every juncture.

I was afraid to inquire about project status with this employee, dreading the ensuing battle. I told myself I didn't want to fire this employee because of the headache it would create.

That's when a smart friend of mine—uninvolved with the business and emotionally detached—clarified things: "Damian, you're already dealing with a headache. And you're paying for it! Why not just make the headache go away?"

Genius. Under any other circumstance I would have seen this obvious solution myself. But I was too close to it. I let emotion harm my enterprise.

Then came clarity from my Vulcan observer. This was, after all, *my* business. That I began on a shoestring budget. That I built and shaped and cried and rejoiced over. Just like it's *your* business, too.

Poor Choices Result in Poorness

You'll make a lot of decisions in running your own business. Never forget, emotional choices are usually poor choices. And poor choices result in poorness.

> Never allow negative emotion to be imposed on you by bad employees or bad customers.

Avoid Big Decisions During Heightened Emotional States

When you're running your own venture, you're always on call. Or as I like to say, "When the self-employed take a day off, all they do is schedule themselves for overtime tomorrow."

Point is, you're going to make decisions about your business even when conditions are less than ideal. If at all possible, avoid making big decisions when you are in a heightened emotional state.

I'm not talking about whether to wear a red or blue sweater kind of decision. I'm talking big-impact stuff.

Likewise, I'm not referring to a heightened emotional state because you just watched the season finale of *This Is Us*. I'm talking life, death, divorce, a kid in the hospital sort of emotional state.

There are phases in life when your ability to make clear-headed decisions is compromised. So don't.

I've cost myself money, pain, and significant setbacks through choices I made when I shouldn't have. Give yourself some separation. If you're like me, you'll think you're tough and don't need it. You do.

Emotioned Out

In August of 2016, my mother died. Don't cry; she was 88. Still, there is an emotional toll in watching your mom wither and die over the course of a month.

I had power of attorney and managed her investments. Which presents additional emotional drainage in managing siblings, relationships, funeral, farm, and the estate. Anyone who's buried a parent understands.

Two months later my brother Mark was diagnosed with pancreatic cancer. I was the first person notified. Mark was my closest sibling and at 12 years older than me, a bit of a father influence. My formative years on the farm were spent with him. He taught me to fish and hunt. We hung out as adults. We drank beer and talked agriculture. I was devastated.

For the next two months, I put things on hold to assist my brother wind down his farming operation. I couldn't focus on my business anyway. We liquidated livestock and sold machinery. We made necessary business arrangements for his land and estate. Every day on the way home, I cried.

Then things went from emotionally draining to stupid. Because I got stupid. While driving across the country, I decided to sell our winter home in Arizona. Mind you, Lori and I had nowhere to go. The scramble to buy new real estate and move was on. To complicate things further, in the middle of all this, my siblings agreed to sell me their shares in my mom's farm.

A few bad decisions later—including walking away from a real estate contract—and we were out $40,000.

I had no business doing all this business at this time. I was emotioned out! My decisions were not crisp. I lost money and created unnecessary distress. Created huge distractions for my business, too.

When the dust settled, I came away with a lesson:

> Never make unnecessary decisions while under distress that add more stress.

Feelings

Humans are emotional beings. You're never going to separate you, your business, and your feelings. But never forget: if you allow emotion to run your business, it will ruin your business!

An Emotional Audit

It's time for you to take a long, hard look at your enterprise and your emotions. Not from your perspective. Do it from Spock's vantage point. No feelings, only logic. Give yourself an audit.

What do you know about you and your emotions?
Where are you allowing your feelings to negatively impact your business?
Does emotion control your decisions?
What decisions are you avoiding because of your feelings?
What relationships should you terminate for your well-being?
  a. Business
  b. Personal
What one action could you take that would make you more prosperous as it pertains to your emotions?

24 You Are Not an Island

You're a rugged individualist. You've made it this far on your own. You've done pretty damn well, if you do say so yourself. You've been making your own decisions since age 16. You've been financially independent since you were 18. Everything you have, you earned. You're self-made.

Does any of this describe you? I'll bet it does. People who start and run their own businesses are independent individuals. That's why they (and you) push themselves (as you push yourself) to do business better. It's who you are.

You're proud of what you've accomplished. With good reason. Please realize, independent as you may be, you're not an island. It's neither healthy, nor productive, to be an island.

We all require support.

You Need Backup!

You make a lot of decisions when you command your own ship. Sometimes you need a second opinion. You need people you can turn to in times of uncertainty. At times, you need people who'll hold your feet to the fire.

The previous chapters outfitted you with an arsenal of weapons. The final piece of the puzzle is putting adequate support in place.

What Is Support?

Support is the battalion of people you surround yourself with in life and business. Who are your people? What do they provide you?

You need an inner circle who'll give you:

- Truth and critical feedback
- Accountability
- Backing when your back's against the wall

Honesty versus Enabling

Truth and critical feedback are two of the main ingredients of support. Sure, you can find "Good Time Charlies" all day long to tell you how awesome you are. When things don't pan out, they tell you it wasn't your fault. When business tanks, you can find people to tell you, "You tried."

Remember what I said about "try"? "Try" is bullshit. "Try" is what weak individuals tell themselves they did when they really didn't. There's no shortage of people who'll tell you you tried, if that's what you want to hear.

I call them Good Time Charlies, but you can refer to them by whatever name you choose. Backslappers, glad-handers . . . these people never have a critical word to say. They tell you you're awesome, just as you are.

The only problem: You're not always awesome just as you are. Sometimes you need a kick in the shorts. Occasionally you need a dose of straight talk to get yourself straight.

Good Time Charlies are really enablers. You don't want enablers in your life or business. They worsen your condition.

Enablers tell bad business operators they're doing everything right even when they're not. "It's not your fault. It's the economy," they tell you.

Enablers avoid the truth for fear the truth might hurt someone's feelings.

Maybe you really did try. And maybe the economy is partly to blame for your failed venture. Whether that's the case or not, your future success requires more than pats on the back. A real supporter pats you on the back, then says, "Here's what you did wrong and here's how we're gonna fix it."

Many corporate boardrooms and C suites are filled with enablers, only there they're called "Yes Men." They ascended to their positions by agreeing with people higher up than them.

Good leaders don't surround themselves with Yes Men and Yes Women. They know the peril of doing so.

In the absence of truth and critical feedback, CEOs or business owners make terrible decisions. All the while being told how brilliant they are by their surrounding cast.

Most folks don't want to hear the truth. They're too weak to digest critical feedback. So they seek out enablers.

Know this: It's impossible to build the life and business you're capable of by surrounding yourself with enablers.

> Never confuse enabling behavior with supportive behavior.

Don't Take That Job

My wife is not an entrepreneurial person by nature. But she knows me. She knows what makes me tick. She delivers truth and critical feedback to keep our ship moving forward.

(continued)

(continued)

In 2001, my political comedy business slowed. Stands to reason. I was a professional Bill Clinton impersonator and Bill left office.

While I fully anticipated a slowdown, I didn't anticipate the hell the next several years would bring. I was developing my next venture, while still delivering a couple shows per month. We had money saved, a healthy investment portfolio, and real estate holdings.

Then came the events of September 11, 2001. You remember the day. Planes took down New York skyscrapers. An airplane hit the Pentagon. Another plane went down in Pennsylvania averting a fourth terrorist attack. Thousands of innocent people were killed.

Two things happened rapidly: Our investments lost half their value. Demand for political comedy vanished.

Over the next several years, Lori and I moved, liquidated assets, pared down expenditures, and scurried to reinvent our next business.

It's difficult for high-energy, entrepreneurial types to go from the fast lane to a bunker mentality. But you do what's necessary given the circumstances.

After four years of setbacks, I decided to throw in the towel. I called every person I knew and asked for an introduction or an interview. After a couple of months, I was offered a sales job.

My wife came home and I told her the news.

"Lori," I said, "it's been four years of fits and starts. We've attempted to buy and start various businesses. Nothing is panning out. I keep changing my act but it's not selling. Apparently, I was just a one-trick pony. We've burned through most of our net worth. I'm not productive and it's driving me crazy. I'm out of ideas. Today, I was offered a position selling medical devices. I'm going back to a normal job."

At this point, my wife demonstrated what real support looks like.

"Damian," she said, "Don't take that job. If you take that job, you'll be good at it. You're a good salesperson and the hardest worker I know. But if you take that job, your spirit will be crushed. Your creativity, your excitement for running your own business, will be gone. I don't want to live with a Damian Mason whose spirit is crushed. Don't take that job!"

If you've ever operated your own enterprise, you understand.

I felt like a failure. After four years of flailing, nothing was working. I thought the answer was to throw in the towel. My wife—and business partner—could have said, "Great, honey, it'll be nice to have a steady paycheck."

But she didn't. She delivered support through truth and critical feedback.

Some people are made to pilot their own creative endeavor. Lori knew this about me. She was willing to provide emotional support so I could keep plunging.

The next day, I felt like a two-ton harness had been lifted off my shoulders. I now knew Lori would support me and my business until I got it right. Within a year, things improved. In two years, business was humming!

(*continued*)

(continued)

Who will give you the support you need to achieve what you are capable of?

> Real support comes from those who care enough about you and your business to be honest.

Accountability

Each of us has the potential to run off the rails from time to time. The cause could be any number of things. A midlife crisis; a family event; a business downturn; or a momentary lapse of laziness. People get derailed.

That's why you need someone (probably multiple someones) to hold you accountable. Peers who hold you accountable are part of your support staff.

Accountability isn't always pretty. Nor is it easy. Which is the reason most people never seek accountability. They don't want to be reminded of what they're doing wrong.

Successful people surround themselves with those who hold them accountable.

Who's Holding You Accountable? I work for myself. I know how easy it is to let projects linger uncompleted. If I didn't accomplish 90% of the things I said I'd do, who'd care? Besides me, who'd even know?

Very likely, it's the same for you.

You could live your life and run your business without setting goals. Most people don't set personal or professional goals.

But, as we've pointed out previously, you're not most people. You want more for yourself. Which is why you need supporters who hold you accountable.

"Better" Requires Daily Practice While some folks get derailed, stagnation is more common. Stagnation occurs when you get too comfortable. You stop pushing yourself. With complacency, your business begins a slow slide into nonexistence.

Do you want to become stagnant? Of course, you don't. This is why you must have people in your corner who hold you to some standards.

Who can you count on to keep you from stagnating?

My friend and fellow speaker, Walter Bond, makes a point about this. He says business professionals are oftentimes lazy. They work at their job, but they don't work at getting better.

Walter was a professional basketball player. He points out that pro athletes spend hours each day in workouts designed to make the athlete better.

A critical component of athletic improvement: coaches who hold the athletes accountable.

If you don't have people in your circle pushing you to get better, hire someone who will. It's that important.

Staying Accountable

Do you have friends who hold you accountable? Most people don't. Who are yours? List them.

_____

_____

_____

(continued)

(continued)

Who holds you accountable at work or in your business?

_____

_____

_____

Which employees, co-workers, or peers can you rely on for truth and critical feedback?

_____

_____

_____

_____

What activities do you regularly undertake to improve yourself/your business?

_____

_____

_____

_____

Coaches, Consultants, and Accountability Partners We live in a world with life coaches, personal consultants, private shamans, and even professional fire walking instructors.

Personally, I have no idea why you'd want to walk on fire, nor do I understand the purpose of doing so. But to each his own.

Before you hire a coach, consultant, or trainer, bear this in mind:

1. An instructor's input is only valuable if you do what you've been instructed to do.
2. Professional advisors are more likely to deliver truth and critical feedback than your friends will.

3. If you hire a professional advisor, be sure the person you are paying has actually accomplished what he or she is advising you to do.

Plenty of people want credit for employing a coach, consultant, or trainer. They want their social circle to know they've employed professional assistance. This is especially true in the world of fitness, incidentally. Some folks have personal trainers but the only sweat they break is flapping their gums talking about their personal trainer.

If you want to get better, build a system of accountability. Those who hold you to standards of achievement are integral elements of your support team.

Your Back's Against the Wall

By now, you may think I'm a hard-ass. I've pointed out the peril of surrounding oneself with enablers. There are, however, times of real need. When your back is against the wall, who are you gonna call?

In the old days, we used to refer to a well-connected person as having a big Rolodex. For the younger demographic, a Rolodex was a desktop tool used to organize one's contacts. Possessing a big Rolodex meant a person had a vast network. Technology replaced the Rolodex but not the need for a good network.

Who is in your Rolodex and what is their role? Most of the people you know and associate with fall into a few categories: customers, business partners, friends, family, or casual acquaintances.

Out of all those categories, only a handful of people will support you when you're up against the wall. Some, because it's their profession—say, legal, financial, or vested business partners. Some, because they love you.

The reality: Most of the people you know won't lift a finger on your behalf, regardless of how bad your circumstance.

That's why it's important to qualify your support before you're backed into a corner.

Your professional support team consists of financial advisors, accountants, bankers, lawyers, business partners, and anyone else who advances your business.

Who are the people on your professional "go-to" support team?

_____

_____

_____

_____

Your personal support circle consists of those folks you can trust with just about anything. These are the people you've been through a war or two with (figuratively speaking). The more successful you become, the harder it is to find people you can trust. Some people are simply looking to exploit their relationship with you for their own benefit.

Who is in your personal support circle?

_____

_____

_____

_____

Two Rules, Even If Your Back's Against the Wall There are two things you must never forget about turning to your emergency supporters.

First, make sure your back is truly against the wall before you declare an emergency. You've heard about *The Boy Who Cried Wolf*, right?

Some people exaggerate the direness of their situation. For these folks, every day is high drama. The only people who respond anymore are their soap opera friends who foster their daily drama. Nobody else listens to these dramatic actors. They've cried wolf one too many times.

Second, remember this old saying: "The only person worthy of a handout is the person who'd never ask for one."

If you are the sort of person who works hard, acts responsibly, and drives your business forward, you probably don't ask for much support. Good for you.

Just realize, things occasionally spin out of control. It's okay to cry wolf when your flock is surrounded by a pack of wolves and you find yourself unarmed!

What Support Isn't

We've established what support looks like and why you need it to thrive. Now let's look at what support *isn't*. Plenty of people get this wrong.

Support is not:

- Enabling people who become disabled as a result of the enabling
- Coddling people so their feelings aren't hurt
- Protecting people from outcomes they should face
- Paying for people who should be financially independent

That last one is a biggie. Too many folks wrongly equate financial "support" with real support. Just remember this:

> People do what they're incentivized to do. If you're paying them to be irresponsible, they'll continue to be irresponsible!

Who's in Your Corner?

Support boils down to surrounding yourself with the right people. You need people who know you so well they can provide truth and critical feedback.

You need people who care enough about you to hurt your feelings if necessary. Honesty isn't always nice. Honesty is just honest. In running your business, you occasionally lose your way. You need someone to point you in the right direction. Even if that means telling you what you don't want to hear.

You need accountability. Because even the most driven of us lose motivation once in a while. Some of our best supporters are those who hold our feet to the fire.

Support can come from those we love. Although oftentimes loved ones pass off enabling behavior as support.

We all need support to achieve what we are capable of. Build your support system. And never, ever mistake enabling, coddling, protecting, or financial gifting as support.

I told you at the beginning of this chapter that none of us are an island. Who's in your corner? Who provides you with honest support?

Do Business Better

I told you in the intro that if you gave me a few hours, I'd save you months or even years in your quest to do business better. I promised a return on your investment of time and money.

To help you reap serious ROI from these pages, we're going to do a brief recap. I'm also going to share my thoughts on the simplicity of success. But first, a word about how this all came together.

Three Conversations

Writing a book isn't physically demanding labor; however, it's still an undertaking. I had notes, stories, ideas, files, and countless examples to share with business-minded individuals such as you. The fuzzy part was knowing exactly what to tell you and how best to share it.

Then I got some good advice from a person more knowledgeable about writing than me: Larry Winget. Larry is a six-time *New York Times/Wall Street Journal* best-selling author. He wrote the foreword to this book. Over cigars and drinks I told him my contemplations. He said, "You know a ton about business. You've run your own successful business. You're on the road speaking to business audiences every week. Just write down what you know and remember who it's for."

The next conversation was with my wife. Lori's insight brought it home. "Damian," she said, "Write the book you wish someone had given you during the first few years running your own business. Something that would have saved you a lot of grief."

The third conversation was a recurring one with myself during bike rides, hikes, and thoughtful moments on airplanes. I asked, "What would I tell people who want to create a successful life and business by choice?"

Success Is Simple, Not Easy

As I contemplated the three conversations, I kept coming back to fundamentals: the traits you cultivate, the habits you establish, and the actions you take yield either success or failure.

I know that sounds simple but just because something is simple doesn't mean it's easy. Running a marathon is simple—it's just running. You started running when you were a little kid. Running is like walking, only faster. So, if running is so simple, why don't more people run marathons? Because running 26.2 miles—simple as the act of running may be—is hard work!

Competitively running 26.2 miles requires strengthening certain personality traits, establishing good habits, and taking daily action through training.

"Wait," you're saying, "Traits, habits, and actions? That sounds like the theme of this book!"

Exactly.

Success is simple, but it's not easy. Your likelihood of success improves with proper instruction. This book is your marathon training.

I titled it *Do Business Better* to keep it simple and to the point. I could have gone the huckster route and called it *How to Be a Billionaire by Sitting on Your Couch.* But when I see this sort of crap, I wonder, "Are people this gullible?" Do people really shell out money to be told success comes without effort, time, risk, or personal investment? Apparently they must.

You didn't shell out money for gimmickry, and I'm too honest to peddle gimmickry. A career on stage taught me to give a smart audience credit. You're a smart audience.

You want success on your terms. You want a better business. I want to help you attain those things.

The Recap

If you apply the lessons from these chapters, you will be wealthier, more productive, and on track to achieving your goals. Guaranteed. The only catch: you have to apply the lessons.

Every chapter asked hard questions. Most chapters had exercises. Did you answer those questions? Did you complete the exercises? Whether you did or didn't, I recommend you revisit the exercises when you're finished reading. It'll make you stronger.

Here is your refresher from each section and chapter.

Traits

The Traits section forced a bit of self-analysis. While you can't change who you are, you can cultivate the traits of success.

You were asked to rate your risk tolerance, from "scaredy cat" to "Evel Knievel." Did you give yourself a rating?

In "Drive," we dissected "busy" versus "productive." We dispelled the talent myth and established that there is no such thing as an ambition gene. More pointedly, what work are you avoiding because it's uncomfortable?

Resilience is the hardest trait to teach and the most critical to building one's own empire. What will you do to become more resilient?

Successful entrepreneurs see opportunities where others see obstacles. What's your purple wall? Visionaries go against the grain, always keeping an eye on the big picture. Do you?

Habits

Routine is mindless and unvarying, whereas habits are intentional behaviors. Do you have good business habits? Where have you allowed yourself to fall into routine?

Most folks are afraid to make a decision so they complicate the matter, pretending there's more complexity than there really is. Be decisive. Pull the trigger. Remember, making no decision *is* a decision.

Everyone says time is money, but few people treat it that way. Where are you investing your entrepreneurial minutes?

You may need a formal business plan to borrow money, but it's certainly not required to make money. Successful people set goals, then attain them.

Realtors are poised to go the way of travel agents. Uber and Lyft are supplanting taxicabs. The marketplace is in constant motion. What are you doing to remain relevant?

When the world looks at you, your product, and your business, what do they see? In "Be Critical," I gave you methods on breaking down tape (the way comedians do) to improve your business.

Coca-Cola spends 11% of revenue on branding initiatives. How much money and effort are you devoting to promoting your business? Wanna thrive tomorrow? Be a promoter today!

Sales, at its core, is understanding a person's problem and positioning yourself as the solution. People overcomplicate the selling process. I recommend you revisit the 10 rules to sales success.

In life and in business, your position is always improved by understanding your position.

Lots of folks would be more prosperous, fit, and happy if only they had the right tools. Makes sense, right? Wrong. That's called the Myth of Inadequate Resources. What lack of accomplishment are you wrongly blaming on scarcity?

Wealth is a habit. You can never build a life and business by choice being financially illiterate. Know money or you'll have no money!

Actions

Whether you're a "solopreneur" or run a business with hundreds of employees, *doing business better* starts with you.

Are you allowing excuses, your background, or toxic relationships to deter your forward progress? We all carry around a certain amount of baggage. It's time to get past what's holding you back.

Everyone possesses a unique business personality. Knowing which of the five P's you gravitate toward will make you more successful. It'll keep you from putting the wrong personality in the wrong position, too.

There are two ways to succeed: Be the best in the world at one thing, or combine your complementary skill sets to create synergies. That's how you exploit your talent stack.

Emotional management is as important to the successful businessperson as financial or employee management. When emotion runs your business, emotion ruins your business.

You are not an island. We all require support. Real support is honest feedback, accountability, and a hand when your back is against the wall. Recognize the difference between support and enabling. Support makes one stronger; enabling makes one weaker.

Do Business Better ─────────────────────────────────

Before you put this book on the shelf, please connect with me on social media, opt in to my newsletter subscriptions, and subscribe to my podcast.

Drop me a note. I'd like to hear about your progress. Let me know which points or illustrations particularly resonated. Alternatively, feel free to tell me where you disagree. You won't hurt my feelings—remember, I started out in comedy!

If you're a member of a professional association or run a company, please consider my services. I earn a living speaking at meetings. I'd love to work with your organization.

Finally, you've heard my mantra about creating a *life* and business by choice. Yet, the word *life* is nowhere to be found in the book title. That's because self-made individuals such as you and me use business to invent the life of our vision.

Sometimes this makes our businesses very personal to us. The connection between life and business is the subject of the final chapter. Enjoy it. Before you do, answer the question I posed in Chapter 1:

What's your definition of success?

_____

_____

_____

Life and Business by Choice

We commonly hear a distinction made between what is business and what is personal. For most of us, the line of demarcation between the two categories gets fuzzy.

Businesses are started, managed, staffed, and patronized by people. That makes business personal.

While my business doesn't define who I am, it's very personal to me. Your business is personal to you, too. That's why throughout this book we touched on the business side as well as the personal side. For every lesson about money and marketing, we discussed the reality of human emotion and personal fortitude.

Like it or not, your professional and private lives commingle. Especially when you're running your own enterprise. It's more difficult to separate yourself from your work when you're the one who created the work.

Everyone struggles with this. Even in the movies.

In *You've Got Mail*, Meg Ryan's character, Kathleen Kelly, makes a valid point regarding the difficulty of separating business from personal. As her family-owned bookstore is being shuttered, Tom Hanks, playing the part of Kathleen's competitor, tells her, "It was business, not personal."

To which she replies, "All that means is it wasn't personal to you. It was personal to me!"

Want another cinematic example? Look at *The Godfather.* Whenever the Corleone family said, "It's not personal, it's strictly business," they killed someone. Actually, they usually killed multiple people.

Okay. From mafia movies and chick flicks, let's get back to your business.

To do business better, you must personally get better.

You'll be amazed at how your professional life and your home life walk in lockstep together. When one improves, generally so does the other. When one is in chaos, they're both in chaos. Humans aren't good at compartmentalizing.

You want a life and business by choice. Now you have the tools and knowledge to create both. No myth of inadequate resources for you!

Successful people enhance their traits, cultivate good habits, and, most importantly, take appropriate action.

In whatever way you define success, I want you to achieve it.

About the Author

Damian Mason is what happens when an entrepreneurial businessperson from an agricultural background collides with a comedian. He's funny, he excels at business, he works like a farmer, and he possesses a keen sense of the marketplace.

Damian knows how to create a life and business by choice because he's done it. From scratch. At age 25, he chucked his sales job with a Fortune 500 company to pursue greater compensation and creativity. It worked. Then his business struggled mightily. Damian reinvented himself. After several iterations and multiple setbacks, his business thrived once again.

Damian speaks to corporations, associations, trade groups, and agricultural organizations. He delivers insights, information, and inspiration in an entertaining package.

Damian is a graduate of Purdue University. He also studied comedy writing and improvisation at The Second City–Chicago. Damian is a member of the Screen Actors Guild and the National Speakers Association.

When he's not traveling for work, Damian can be found on his Indiana farm with his wife, Lori, or escaping from winter at their Arizona residence. Damian loves the outdoors, his wife, his dog, his beer, and his independence.

Connect with Damian at www.damianmason.com

Facebook: @DamianMasonProfessionalSpeaker
LinkedIn: Damian Mason
Twitter: @DamianPMason

Index